CASE STUDIES IN
CULTURAL ANTHROPOLOGY

GENERAL EDITORS

George and Louise Spindler

STANFORD UNIVERSITY

SAMOAN VILLAGE

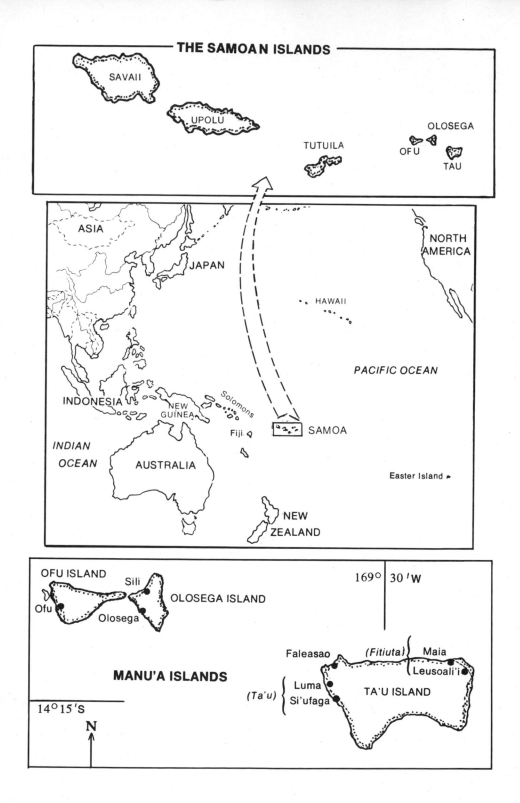

THE SAMOAN ISLANDS

SAVAII

UPOLU

TUTUILA

OLOSEGA

OFU

TAU

ASIA

JAPAN

NORTH AMERICA

HAWAII

PACIFIC OCEAN

INDONESIA

NEW GUINEA

Solomons

Fiji

SAMOA

INDIAN OCEAN

AUSTRALIA

Easter Island ▸

NEW ZEALAND

OFU ISLAND

Sili

OLOSEGA ISLAND

Ofu

Olosega

169° 30′W

MANU'A ISLANDS

Faleasao

(Fitiuta)

Maia

Leusoali'i

(Ta'u)

Luma

Si'ufaga

TA'U ISLAND

14°15′S

N

SAMOAN VILLAGE #b

By
LOWELL DON HOLMES
Wichita State University

HOLT, RINEHART AND WINSTON, INC.

NEW YORK   CHICAGO   SAN FRANCISCO   ATLANTA
DALLAS   MONTREAL   TORONTO   LONDON   SYDNEY

Cover photograph: *An untitled man preparing food for the chiefs.*

Library of Congress Cataloging in Publication Data

Holmes, Lowell Don, 1925-
Samoan village.

(Case studies in cultural anthropology)
Bibliography: p. 109
1. Fitiuta, American Samoa.   2. Ethnology—Samoan
Islands—Case studies.   I. Title. I. Series.
DU819.F58H65   301.29'96'13   74-1294
ISBN 0-03-077925-1

Foreword

ABOUT THE SERIES

These case studies in cultural anthropology are designed to bring to students, in beginning and intermediate courses in the social sciences, insight into the richness and complexity of human life as it is lived in different ways and in different places. They are written by men and women who have lived in the societies they write about and who are professionally trained as observers and interpreters of human behavior. The authors are also teachers, and in writing their books they have kept the students who will read them foremost in their minds. It is our belief that when an understanding of ways of life very different from one's own is gained, abstractions and generalizations about social structure, cultural values, subsistence techniques, and the other universal categories of human social behavior become meaningful.

ABOUT THE AUTHOR

Lowell D. Holmes is professor and former chairman of the Department of Anthropology at Wichita State University, Wichita, Kansas. He holds a doctorate in anthropology from Northwestern University (1957) where he studied under Professors William R. Bascom, Francis L. K. Hsu, and Melville J. Herskovits. Dr. Holmes has conducted field research in American Samoa in 1954, 1962–3, and 1974, and he also maintains a continuing research interest in American culture. His publications include *Ta'u, Stability and Change in a Samoan Village* (1958), *The Story of Samoa* (1967), *Anthropology, An Introduction*, second edition (1971), *Aging and Modernization* (1972), and numerous articles on Polynesian culture in major anthropological journals. Dr. Holmes also produced a documentary film on Fitiuta entitled *Fa'a Samoa: The Samoan Way* (1970). He is a Fellow of the American Anthropological Society, a member of the Polynesian Society and Sigma Xi, and a former president of the Central States Anthropological Society.

ABOUT THE BOOK

The Samoan islands is one of those places where most Americans think they would like to go. The pleasant climate and people are legendary, and the islands have been made famous by the many writings about them, not the least of which is Margaret Mead's well known *Coming of Age in Samoa.* This case study by Lowell Holmes is an informative, straightforward, and interestingly written descriptive analysis of one village in the Manu'a group of American Samoa. The reader who finishes this case study, and once started most will, should still be motivated to go to Samoa, but his or her expectations will be tempered by a cautious appraisal of reality.

European contact with Samoa, insofar as it is recorded, occurred first in 1722, though there is some evidence that contact may have occurred prior to this date, but by only a few years. The first mission was established in 1828 and American involvement began in 1839. The Manu'a group of American Samoa was officially incorporated as a United States territorial holding in 1904. All of Samoa, including American Samoa, has therefore had long-term and rather intensive contact with the West. Despite this, Samoa has been able to retain much of its traditional culture while other Pacific peoples have to a great extent lost theirs. Within a conservative culture, the Manu'a group of islands and the village of Fitiuta have remained particularly conservative. The reasons for this conservatism are dealt with in the case study. Whatever values one may place upon cultural conservatism in a changing world, the fact of this conservatism, in the place studied by Lowell Holmes, makes it possible to describe Samoan culture and social structure as a living entity.

The case study will give the reader a working knowledge of the basic elements of traditional Samoan culture as it is lived out today, including subsistence; use of traditional materials, structures, and shelters; the principles of rank and the elaboration of roles in the context of different groups; title succession; Talking Chiefs; ceremonies; decision-making; the spiritual world; and the life cycle. The case study is characterized by a happy balance between structural or technical analyses and enlivened descriptions of scenes and events in which the significant features of the more formal and abstract analysis are demonstrated.

Samoan culture, though comparatively stable, is of course changing, and in recent years changing more rapidly than before. The most important changes began when the acceptance of Christianity meant abolishing polygamy, divorce, political marriages, adultery, premarital sex, lavish gift exchanges at marriages, public tests of virginity, prostitution, nudity, liquor, gambling, tattooing, and sorcery. The ways in which the people adapted to what could have been a very disruptive confrontation between native Samoan and Christian belief and practice are described. The description of culture change in the last decade or so, however, raises ominous questions that do not appear to be easily answered. Samoan villages are having difficulties that are being experienced everywhere modernization is taking place. The environment is deteriorating, and sewage and trash disposal is becoming a severe problem. Wage work is displacing a subsistence economy. Many thousands of Samoans have migrated to the United States, particularly to the West Coast. The conclusion of the case study really raises the question that is now becoming universal and applicable to the highly developed industrial societies, such as that of the United States, as well as to those that are in the process of modernization: Is modernization worth the price? For some Samoans, and some of them live in the village of Fitiuta, the answer may well be "no."

George and Louise Spindler
General Editors

Phlox, Wisconsin

Preface

This account of Samoan culture is based on data collected during field trips to American Samoa in 1954 (eleven months) and 1962–1963 (fifteen months) plus a four week visit in January 1974 to study the effects of educational television in the Tutuila village schools. My earliest trip, in which I did a methodological restudy of the work of Margaret Mead, Felix Keesing, and Sir Peter Buck, was sponsored by the University of Hawaii under the Tri-Institutional Pacific Program, while the later research, a study of village leadership and decision-making, was supported by the National Science Foundation.

My research in 1954 concentrated exclusively on Manu'an culture, and while I resided in Ta'u village, the site of Margaret Mead's 1925–1926 study of adolescent girls, frequent trips were made to Fitiuta, and my principal informant claimed Fitiuta as his home village. Shortly after my visit, he was elected to the High Chief title of Iliili in that village. My 1962–1963 study was broader in scope, and in addition to work in Manu'a I also studied three communities on the island of Tutuila.

Initial entrance into Samoan society was accomplished through the help of High Chief Tufele, holder of one of the two highest ranking titles in Fitiuta. My wife, daughter, and I lived in his house in Ta'u, and I occasionally visited his family in Fitiuta. Tufele's wife aided me in the selection of my first key informant, and members of the Tufele family in Ta'u made life comfortable for us by providing a large portion of our food and by taking care of a variety of household chores associated with living in traditional Samoan housing.

My first trip to Fitiuta was made in the company of the Crown Prince of Tonga (now King), and because of this fortunate circumstance I was able to observe some of the most elaborate protocol ever accorded visitors to Manu'a. While I spent only a few days in Manu'a in this regal company, it proved to be a great asset to my work when I arrived several weeks later to take up extended residence. At this time I was often referred to as "the *palagi* who came with the Tuitonga," and this was a considerable advantage in establishing rapport with high-ranking Manu'an chiefs.

In Samoa it is important to first gain the acceptance of the men of rank, and once this has been done, one has fairly free access to all the members of the society. The age and sex of the anthropologist also has a bearing on one's ability to establish rapport. Samoa is somewhat of a male-oriented society, and most important ceremonials are attended almost entirely by men. Whatever success I had in studying this society may also be attributed to the fact that I was accompanied in the field by my wife and daughter. Although the chiefs thought me a bit young (twenty-nine), the fact that I was a husband and a father qualified me as an adult and therefore worthy of some of their time and information.

My presence in the society was explained by stating that I was a teacher whose students wanted to learn how the people of the South Seas lived. Samoans have great respect for education, and teachers have high prestige. These people also have an understanding of what a teacher of anthropology does, and they refer to such a person as *a'oa'o aganu'u* (one who studies the customs of the country). I also stated that I was there to collect information so I could write a history of Samoan life. On my second trip in 1962–1963 the Samoans thought this project particularly relevant since there was a growing awareness that traditional Samoan culture was rapidly disappearing. Many of the people expressed gratitude that someone was interested in recording the particulars of their way of life so future generations would be able to read about how their ancestors lived. We both agreed therefore that we had to be very careful about the accuracy of the information.

A large variety of informants was used, some tradition-oriented and some highly acculturated. One man who worked with me on matters relating to village leadership and decision-making held a bachelor's degree in political science from Drake University, while a number of the older chiefs in Fitiuta had little or no education and spoke no English. Village schoolteachers often proved to be good informants, particularly those who had been born and raised in Manu'a. One such man had an interest in ethnography himself and had for years been collecting myths, legends, poetry (*solo*), genealogies, bush medicine remedies, and other traditional lore. All of this information had been written down in a set of record books. He served as a kind of library for the Talking Chiefs of his family who wanted to improve their knowledge of *fa'asamoa* (Samoan custom) and therefore their oratorical effectiveness. Specialists were also consulted for particular kinds of information not generally shared throughout the society. Several days were spent with carpenters building a guest house. I photographed their activities and spent a good deal of time interrogating them concerning proper materials, methods, and traditions relative to their craft.

If we have been successful in writing the proposed "history of Samoan life," it has been largely due to the cooperation and interest of the people of Manu'a. It became a common experience to have a young messenger come to our house at all hours of the day or night and inform us that "something important" was happening somewhere in the village that we should be sure to witness.

During our stay in Manu'a in 1954, our year-old daughter became seriously ill and had to be taken by interisland vessel to the hospital in Pago Pago. The boat arrived, but the surf was higher than it had been in many weeks. The Samoans said that there was only one man who could safely guide the longboat through the heavy surf and reach the vessel. This man, Upega, was ill and could barely use his legs. When Upega heard about our crisis, he instructed the members of his household to carry him to the longboat. He took the sweep oar, and as the boat moved out toward the line of breakers, he counted the waves and at just the right moment gave the oarsmen the order to pull with all their strength. The boat plunged through two lines of breaking waves and then found smooth water. Behind us a great cheer went up from what appeared to be everyone in the village wishing us well. It is to these warm and gentle people that I dedicate this book.

L. D. H.

Contents

SAMOAN VILLAGE

1 / The village—race, language, and cultural history

The sky offshore was a brilliant blue, but on the island of Ta'u, near the summit of the mountain known as Lata, great pillows of clouds were building up as the moisture-laden trade winds climbed higher and higher on its slopes. As they neared the top of the 3056 foot peak, the wetness of the winds was turned to white. Buoyed by these gentle drafts, a gull wheeled and soared, a thousand feet or more above the white line of surf which marked the reef. From this altitude the houses of the village of Fitiuta, sheltered as they were in a long valley extending inland from the beach, resembled little more than irregular strings of somber beads. Those shaped round or oval were the thatched domes of traditional Samoan *fales*, while the rectangular ones were the rusting galvanized roofs of *palagi* (European) styled structures. Mostly the shapes were round.

The village stretched more than a mile and a quarter into its cradling valley, the exact length of a concrete sidewalk that served as the village's central thoroughfare. The walkway, scarcely wide enough for two people to pass, was flanked at irregular intervals by Samoan dwellings with grounds landscaped with hibiscus bushes, *pua* gardenia trees, and decorative green and yellow *lautalotalo* plants. A carpet of well-kept grass covered the valley floor making the entire village appear like a well-planned park or perhaps even Hollywood's idea of an idyllic South Sea settlement.

Actually the village of Fitiuta is made up of two hamlets—Maia and Leusoali'i. While the residents of each are quick to claim their separate affiliation and while each hamlet has its own group of chiefs which rules on local issues, there is also a "Great Council," known as the *fono faleula tau aitu*, wherein chiefs of the many families of both Maia and Leusoali'i meet together and cooperate in matters of government business and local affairs which concern them all. The visitor to this community would hardly be aware of the division of Fitiuta, for the two hamlets share a dispensary building, a school house, and a church. There is community-owned land planted in coconuts which all work cooperatively, and both hamlets utilize the same boat house, copra shed, and surf boats.

The people of Fitiuta are very proud of their community, for legends and myths—repeated throughout the whole of the Samoan archipelago—relate that it was here in a place called Saua that the god Tagaloa chose to create the first

1

Fitiuta fales *and village cement walkway.*

human being and crown the first human king, the Tuimanu'a. It was also near Fitiuta, so the myths say, that the first kava ceremony was performed, and it was from here that the first couples were sent forth by Tagaloa to settle the many islands of Polynesia which the god had created as stepping stones across the Pacific. This pride in living on the site of such important ancient events is reflected in the fact that Fitiuta today remains more traditionally Samoan in its village organization, ceremonial commitment, and even in its language than most villages of American Samoa. The people of Fitiuta retain the traditional *t* sound in their speech, while most other inhabitants of Samoa have replaced it with a *k*. Thus, to most outsiders the name of this ancient village is Fikiuka. Village pride is also reflected in its immaculate appearance and stable social and political structure. For many, Fitiuta is the epitome of *fa'asamoa* (the Samoan way).

Entree to the village is by way of its beach on the north side of the island of Ta'u. Here a boat passage has been blasted through the coral reef and here is where the boathouse for the village *fa'atasi* (surf or longboats) stands. Near the boathouse is the village copra shed where bags of coconut kernel are stored awaiting the weekly visit of the interisland motor vessel.

Once past the narrow strip of white sand beach the concrete walkway begins. It seems strangely incongruous in this indigenous South Sea setting. For the citizens of Fitiuta, however, it is another source of pride, a product of local financing and labor. The walkway negotiates a gentle slope leading up into the hamlet of Maia.

It leads past the village lands and houses of chiefs[1] La'apui, Paopao, Nūnū, and Sega, past the London Missionary Society (now Congregational Church of Samoa) chapel, the village school and the home of the *faifeau* (pastor), and then enters the hamlet of Leusoali'i and traverses the household lands of chiefs Ale, Ili, Pomele, and Moa. Then the sidewalk ends and a well-used dirt path continues on through plantation lands and eventually winds its way down to the sea in a place known as Saua, the mythical Samoan Garden of Eden.

In the heat of midday, Fitiuta is a sleepy village. The humid, sultry air hangs heavy, and even the smoke from the cooking fires seems to ascend slowly and with difficulty. Most of the villagers have sought the shade of their *fales*, and there is little movement on the village path. Now and then a teenager emerges from a house to fetch water or to retrieve a toddler, and there is activity in the school building near the heart of the village, but most of the people of Fitiuta, particularly the men, are resting, for they have already put in the better part of a day's work. The men have risen well before dawn and travelled several miles to clear agricultural lands, to plant, weed, or harvest, and they have earned their rest. In some of the houses small groups of women sit cross-legged on the mat-covered floors and converse softly as they weave pandanus mats or embroider floral designs on pillow cases. Behind many of the main household buildings a handful of young men and women tend the cooking fires where taro, bananas, breadfruit, and occasionally bundles of leaves containing fish are being prepared for the evening meal. After an hour's cooking, the food is removed from the beds of heated rocks with bamboo tongs and placed in woven baskets to cool. In the *fales* near the school it is more difficult for the men to rest, for education in Samoa is a noisy business requiring unison recitation of English words and sentences and answers to arithmetic problems.

Rising on either side of the village are steep slopes which at their summits flatten out to plateaus containing agricultural lands owned by Fitiuta families and uncleared sections owned communally by the village. On these plateaus are found the major stands of coconut trees as well as quantities of banana and breadfruit trees. Some taro may be found in this area, but the main beds are found further from the village and higher on the mountain sides where the land is more fertile.

The village of Fitiuta is but one of three settlements on the island of Ta'u. The community of Faleasao lies some five or six miles to the west over mountain trails, and a mile beyond that is the village of Ta'u—the largest on the island, with a population of better than 700.

Seven miles to the northwest of the island of Ta'u are two small islets, Ofu and Olosega. At low tide it is possible to wade from one to the other. Taken together they have but four square miles of land area and only a small fraction of this is cultivable. Although the total land area of Ofu and Olosega is but one-fourth the

[1] Titled men (*matai*) in Samoa are generally called "chiefs" (lower case), but chiefs may be of two types—"Chiefs" and "Talking Chiefs" (using capitals with these titles). If referring to a titled man in general lower case is used, but if reference is made to a particular kind of chief capitals are used.

size of the island of Ta'u, the two islets contain three villages. The village of Ofu has a population of 289, approximately equal to that of Olosega village. Sili, also on the island of Olosega, has but 99 people.

The three islands, Ta'u, Ofu, and Olosega, are collectively known as the Manu'a Group of American Samoa and make up the most easterly extension of the Samoan archipelago. There is a small atoll called Muliava (Rose Island) lying another eighty miles east of Ta'u, but this outlier is uninhabited.

Travelling sixty miles westward from the island of Ta'u one encounters the largest insular territory in American Samoa, Tutuila, with the famous port of Pago Pago and a total indigenous population of approximately 27,000. This island, with its fifty-seven villages, is roughly eighteen miles long and six miles wide. The land is mountainous and most of its villages are located along its irregular coastline. One ridge of mountains (actually the remains of an ancient volcanic crater) partially encloses Pago Pago Bay, one of the largest and best protected harbors in the Pacific. Tutuila, the tiny island of Aunu'u (just off the eastern tip of Tutuila), and the Manu'a Group make up the Territory of American Samoa, a possession of the United States since 1900.

Forty miles west of Tutuila is the island of Upolu and ten miles beyond that is Savai'i. These, plus two islets, Manono and Apolima, constitute the independent nation of Western Samoa. Prior to Western Samoa's independence, which came in 1961, this country's 134,478 people and 1097 square miles of land were governed by New Zealand under a trusteeship charter of the United Nations.

Western Samoa is agriculturally more productive than American Samoa. It's great expanses of farm land yield substantial quantities of cash crops such as copra, cocoa, and bananas. Western Samoa's capital and principal port, Apia, has a relatively poor harbor compared to Pago Pago but manages to carry on a significant volume of international trade in agricultural products.

Apia gives the impression of being a more naturally evolved South Sea community than Pago Pago since the latter began as a naval base and still retains that flavor under the control of the United States Department of Interior.

The Samoan archipelago, which lies in a general east-west direction at 14 degrees south latitude and between 168 and 173 degrees west longitude, is volcanic in origin and is of relatively recent creation (late Pliocene to mid-Pleistocene). All of the islands in the chain have much in common topographically. There are low coastal areas with sand beaches (where the majority of villages are located) and then the land rises abruptly to highland ridges. Nearly all of the coastline is fringed with coral reefs. On the island of Savai'i, mountain summits reach an altitude of 6000 feet, but on the island of Tutuila the highest peak is Matafao, with an altitude of 2141 feet.

Since this region is tropical, with warm temperatures and abundant rainfall (averaging 150 inches per year), vegetation is dense and green. Bushes, ferns, grasses, and vines carpet the mountain slopes beneath stands of high quality timber such as *ifi lele* (*Intsis bijuga*), *tavai* (*Rhustaitenis*), and *asi* (*Syzygium inophyl-*

loides). Mountain tops are clothed in mosses, lichens, and ferns, and there is a general absence of trees.

The animal population of the archipelago, aside from domesticated varieties—chickens, pigs, dogs, and a handful of horses and cattle—is meager. There are a few wild bush pigs, two species of nonpoisonous snakes, a dozen varieties of lizards (including the gecko), and land crabs. Fruit bats (*Pteropus ruficollis*), sometimes referred to as "flying foxes," are common, as is the small Polynesian rat (*Rattus exulans Peale*). While this rodent probably arrived in Samoa with the original settlers, the large wharf rat (*Rattus norvegicus*) found around port towns is of recent introduction, having arrived on European vessels. There are thirty-four species of land birds including such game fowl as the golden plover, wild duck, and three varieties of pigeon. The most important bird culturally is a small green parakeet, the *sega*, with red markings, that is referred to as the "chief's bird." Its colorful feathers are used to decorate the Samoan's most prized possession, the finemat.

Insects are numerous in this tropical climate, but only two cause serious problems. The mosquito (*Stegomzia pseudoscatellaris*) is a carrier of filariasis, the disease which in its advanced stages develops into elephantiasis. There is no malaria in Samoa. The rhinoceros beetle (*Oryctes rhinoceros*), on the other hand, is a costly pest in that it destroys the coconut palm. Two varieties of centipede and a single variety of scorpion are present in the archipelago. Their bites, while painful, are seldom fatal. Cockroaches, which often attain a length of two inches, are annoying creatures which persist in destroying clothing and finemats. Flies are present in abundance and are a serious health hazard, for they breed in human waste matter on the beaches or in the bush.

PHYSICAL TYPE

Culturally (and geographically) the Samoan people are identified as Western Polynesians, a category they share with the inhabitants of Tonga, Niue, the Tokelaus, and to a certain extent with the people of the Fiji Islands. Although there are cultural similarities and numerous historical traditions concerning political interaction between Samoans and Fiji Islanders, the two are markedly different in physical type. While Fijians are usually classified as Oceanic Negroes and related to Melanesians to the west of them, Samoans are Polynesian in physical type and thus constitute a racially hybrid group exhibiting a blend of physical characteristics. The Polynesian physical type has been described by W. W. Howells as follows:

> The Polynesians are tall and rather like the Whites in body form, though a little more solid. In this, but mainly in the head and face, they strongly suggest a mixture of Mongoloid and White, with possibly a little Negroid causing occasional frizzy hair. This is going by appearances; we do not know what actually went into the recipe, but it is hard to mistake the force of the White

elements. The Polynesians have large, deep faces, with noses both long and broad and eyes without Mongoloid folds. Skin is light brown to brown, but hair is wavy, and beards are usual (1967:329).

Some claim that Samoans resemble Europeans more closely than any other group of Polynesians. The color of their skin is a medium yellowish brown and their hair is black or dark brown and wavy or straight in form. Samoans are relatively tall, with men averaging five feet seven and one half inches and women five feet three inches. Faces are broad with straight noses of medium breadth, dark brown eyes, and full but not protruding lips.

LANGUAGE

The language of Samoa is a dialect of the linguistic family known as Austronesian (formerly called Malayo-Polynesian). It has further been placed in the subgroup Samoic, a category which also includes the languages spoken by the inhabitants of the Tokelau and Ellice Islands, Eastern Futuna, and Tikopia. It is a pleasant sounding language because of its liberal use of vowels and has often been referred to as the "Italian of the Pacific." Roger Green (1966:34) maintains that Samoan was one of the earlier established languages of Polynesia although of more recent development than Fijian or Tongan.

Samoan has only nine consonants: *p, t, f, v, s, m, n, g* (pronounced *ng*), and *l*. The five basic vowels used by English-speakers—*a, e, i, o, u*—are augmented in Samoan speech by the use of long vowel sounds. For example, *tama* (boy) ends in a short *a* and is pronounced *tahm-uh*, but the word for "father" is *tamā* (long vowel indicated by the accent mark above the letter *a*) and is pronounced *tahm-ah*. As is true of most Polynesian languages, every consonant in Samoan is separated by one or more vowels as may be seen in the following sentence: *O le ā o fafine a tata lavalava i le vaitafo.* (The women will go to wash clothes in the river.) Furthermore, there is the feature of the glottal stop (indicated by ') which is a choking off of sound as in words like Savai'i, Ta'u, Manu'a, or *va'a* (boat). This interruption of sound is phonemically very important, as a similarly spelled word without the glottal stop has a very different meaning. For example, *fai* means "do," and *fa'i* means "banana"; *sao* means "to escape," and *sa'o* means "straight."

Samoan has a smaller vocabulary than English, but then Samoan culture is somewhat less complex, at least technologically. Its basic stock of morphemes is often called upon to do yeoman service in satisfying the society's communication needs. The word *lau*, for example, has nine meanings: "leaf," "lip," "brim of a cup," "thatch," "breadth," "hundred," "your," "fish drive," and "to sing a song verse by verse."

A characteristic feature of the Samoan language is its use of compound nouns which are formed by the root noun plus some other part of speech which qualifies its meaning. The Samoan word meaning "store" (*faleoloa*), for example, is compounded from the noun *fale* meaning "building" and the noun *oloa* meaning "goods." The word for "orator" (*failauga*) combines the verb *fai* (to make) with the noun *lauga* (speech). The Samoan word for "wickedness" (*agaleaga*) is compounded by pairing the noun *aga* (conduct) with the adjective *leaga* (bad).

Verbs also differ markedly from those found in the English language. The tense of the verb, for example, is never indicated by the form of the verb itself. Verb spellings remain the same for past, present, or future. In order to indicate tense, Samoan speakers add what might be called verbal particles. Examples of these are *O lo'o*, which expresses continuous action in the present as in *O lo'o galue Ioane* (John is working.); *Sa* or *Na*, expressing the past tense as in *Sa e alu i Fitiuta māsina talu ai?* (Did you go to Fitiuta last month?); and *O le ā*, expressing the definite future as in *O le ā timu.* (It will rain.).

The most unique feature of the Samoan language is the special set of honorific terms known as the "chief's language." This is a class of polite or respectful words which are substituted for ordinary words when one is speaking to someone of chiefly rank. For example, an untitled man has an *'aiga* (meal), but a chief has a *taumafataga*; an untitled person puts his hat on his *ulu* (head), but a chief places it on his *ao*; an untitled person may become *ma'i* (ill), but a chief becomes *gasegase*; and a chief may *maliu* (die), but a commoner will merely *oti*.

ORIGINS—THE ANTHROPOLOGICAL VIEW

The origin of the people of Samoa is a matter of some debate in anthropological circles. As we have pointed out, their language is a branch of the Austronesian family, a language stock spoken by Pacific peoples from Easter Island to the southeast Asian mainland, and their physical type is strongly Asiatic. While most anthropologists reject the Thor Heyerdahl "Kon Tiki" theory—that Samoans as well as other Polynesians are of New World origin—the exact chronology, routes, and methods of migration of all Polynesian peoples out of the Old World are only recently becoming clear. At one time anthropologists postulated mass migrations of maritime-oriented people out of southern China or Southeast Asia with cultural systems already of the Polynesian type. These migrations were assumed to have been through the islands of Micronesia or past New Guinea and other eastern Melanesian islands with the first long-term settlement taking place in Samoa or the Tonga Islands. Subsequent migrations out of Samoa or Tonga led to the peopling of the Cook Islands, French Polynesia, Hawaii, Easter Island, and New Zealand.

Today, as a result of substantial linguistic evidence and a smattering of archeological data, most Pacific specialists believe that the voyagers from Southeast Asia (physically resembling the present-day inhabitants of Indo-China) moved slowly out into the Pacific until they had settled the uninhabited Melanesian islands to the east of New Guinea (for example, the Solomons, New Hebrides, Loyalty Islands, New Caledonia, and Fiji Islands) by 1500 B.C. These migrants had a Neolithic-type culture with domesticated plants (taro and yams), domesticated animals (pigs, chickens, and dogs), and skills such as pottery making and barkcloth manufacture.

By the first century A.D. the Samoan islands had been settled by emigrants from eastern Melanesia. The diffusion of dark-skinned people into the islands of eastern Melanesia did not take place until fairly late in time. Archeological evidence suggests that negroid-type people (probably from New Guinea) did not arrive in the Fiji Island area until about 1000 A.D. Physical anthropologist W. W. Howells (1933:335) suggests that since Fijians differ in physical type from Samoans only in their slightly shorter faces, somewhat darker pigmentation, and broader, flatter noses that the introduction of negroid physical traits into the originally Samoan–Tongan-type population of Fiji did not occur until as late as the eleventh century A.D.

ORIGINS—THE SAMOAN MYTHOLOGICAL VIEW

The Samoans have their own explanation of where they came from, and it differs significantly from that of the anthropologists. The Samoan myth of creation, still passed on from generation to generation, reads as follows:

In the beginning there·were only the heavens and the waters covering the earth. The god Tagaloa looked down from his place in the sky and considered creating a place on the earth where he could stand. So he made a resting place by creating the rock called Manu'atele (Greater Manu'a). Tagaloa was pleased with his work and said, "It would be well to have still another resting place." He divided the rock Manu'atele so he would have other places in the sea that would serve as stepping stones. From these pieces of rock he created Savai'i, Upolu, Tonga, Fiji, and the other islands which lie scattered about the wide ocean.

When Tagaloa had finished fashioning all of these islands, he returned to Samoa. He measured the distance between the islands of Savai'i and Manu'a and found it to be too great. So he placed a rock half-way between and designated it as a place of repose for the chiefs. He called this last island Tutuila.

Tagaloa then sent a sacred vine to spread over the rocks. The leaves of the sacred creeper fell off and decayed and things like worms grew from them. Tagaloa saw that the creeper had given birth to worms which had neither heads, nor legs, nor breath of life. So the god came down and provided these worms with heads, legs, arms, and a beating heart. Thus the worms became men. Tagaloa took a male and female and placed them on each of the islands that he had created. The man Sa and the woman Vai'i were placed on one island and the place was called Savai'i. U and Polu were placed on another and it became known as Upolu. The couple Tutu and Ila were the first inhabitants of Tutuila. To and Ga went to a place that Tagaloa named Toga (Tonga), and Fi and Ti were taken to the place to be called Fiti (Fiji).

Then Tagaloa decided that men should be appointed to rule the different islands and so he created the title of Tui (king). He created the titles Tuiaga'e, Tuita'u,

Tuiofu, Tuiolosega, Tuiatua, Tuia'ana, Tuitoga, and Tuifiti and thus established lords of the islands.

Then Tagaloa looked upon all he had created and decided that there should be a king greater than all the others and that he should reside in Manu'atele, his first creation. He selected the son of Po (night) and Ao (day) to be the king of kings. When this boy was to be born it was found that his abdomen was firmly attached to his mother's womb. Because of this he was given the name Satia i le Moaatoa (attached by the abdomen), and the whole island group which would be his domain received the name Samoa (sacred abdomen). When the child was born he sustained a great wound as he was ripped from his mother's body. From this came the name of the place of his birth, Manu'atele (the great wound). When this boy grew to manhood he became the king of all the Tui (kings) and carried the title Tuimanu'a Moaatoa.

ORIGIN OF THE NAME OF FITIUTA

Legend has it that Fitiuta was originally known as Aga'e. In ancient days it was the residence of the first Samoan chief, Tagaloa Ui, a mortal descended from the gods. His daughter Sina was renown throughout the islands for her beauty. When the King of Fiji (Tuifiti) heard of this comely and noble young woman he travelled to Samoa to propose marriage. Since Sina met all of the king's expectations, a marriage was arranged and Sina returned to Fiji with her royal husband. In Fiji, Sina lived in the king's mountain retreat with all the luxuries she could possibly desire, but she was very lonely, for the king was usually away attending to affairs of state.

Tagaloa Ui heard that his daughter was lonely, and he sent his eldest son Taeotagaloa to visit her. After meeting with Sina the young man went before the Fijian king and told him of his intention to return to Samoa with his sister because she was unhappy with her lonely life among foreign peoples so far from her homeland.

While Tuifiti was sad to hear that his young queen wished to leave, he agreed that the decision was hers to make, and he would not prevent her from leaving. The king did, however, make one request. He said that when Sina returned to Samoa she should take the name of her Fijian mountain village and the many crops that grow there as his gift to her and the Samoan people.

When Sina arrived in Manu'a, Tagaloa Ui met her and asked what she had brought from Fiji. She showed him the Fijian plants (among which was a variety of breadfruit which bears every month and not just twice or three times a year), and she told him that she had brought a new name for their village of Aga'e. Thus the village became known as Fitiuta, which means "Fiji in the mountains," and because of the fine plants which Sina introduced, the village has never known famine.

THE COMING OF THE WHITE MAN

The first documented contact between Europeans and Samoan islanders took place on June 14, 1722, when Admiral Jacob Roggeveen, commanding two ships in an exploratory voyage for the Dutch West India Company, sighted the Manu'a Island group and hove to off the village of Ta'u. Whether or not the villagers had ever seen such vessels before is debatable, but if they felt fear at seeing these tall ships, it was easily eclipsed by their curiosity, for they launched an outrigger, brought it alongside Roggeveen's ship, and climbed aboard. Once on board they produced coconuts which were traded to the ship's company for six rusty nails. After about a two-hour visit, the Samoans departed leaving the impression in Roggeveen's mind that they were

> a harmless good sort of people, and very brisk and likely; for they treated each other with visible markes of civility, and had nothing in their behavior that was wild or savage. Their bodies were not painted . . . but were clothed from the girdle downwards, with a kind of silk fringes very neatly folded.

From Ta'u, Roggeveen and company sailed some seven miles to the twin islands of Ofu and Olosega where an outrigger canoe containing "the High Chief of Ofu village" and his *taupou* (ceremonial village virgin) came out to meet the ship's longboat which had been rowed to a point just beyond the fringe reef. During his parley with ship's officers the chief pointed to a blue necklace worn by the *taupou* and indicated that he would like another like it. When the boat crew made it clear that they did not have one to trade the negotiations were quickly terminated, but not with hostility. Since Roggeveen seems to indicate that Manu'a islanders were familiar with iron nails and since the *taupou* was wearing a common trade item of the day, there is reason to believe that Captain Roggeveen and his crew were not the Samoan islanders' first European visitors.

Manu'a islanders did not see European ships or men again for forty-six years. On May 3, 1768, the French navigator Louis Antoine DeBougainville, commanding the ships *La Boudeuse* and *L'Etoile*, sighted the Manu'a group and established contact with the inhabitants of Ofu and Olosega. Here he traded bits of red cloth for yams, coconuts, barkcloths, lances, and "bad" fishhooks. According to his account, these Samoans were not interested in nails, knives, or earrings—trade items which he had found very much in demand in Tahiti. While DeBougainville was much impressed with Samoans as sailors and boat builders—naming their archipelago the "Navigator's Islands"—his opinion of them as people was somewhat less favorable than that of Roggeveen. DeBougainville states that they were not as gentle as Tahitians and that "we were always obliged to be upon our guard against their cunning tricks to cheat us by their barter."

After leaving Manu'a DeBougainville sailed past Tutuila and probably Upolu. While none of DeBougainville's men landed on any of the islands, trading with natives in outrigger canoes occurred at several places.

The first Europeans to set foot on Samoan soil were members of the La Perouse expedition. For this they paid dearly with thirteen lives. On December 6, 1787, the frigates *Boussole* and *Astrolabe* sighted the Manu'a group where they traded with the people of Olosega Island (again at sea) before continuing on to Tutuila. Since La Perouse's ships needed fresh water and the people of Manu'a had proved to be friendly, La Perouse decided to land at the village of Fagasā, on the north coast of Tutuila. Captain M. DeLangle, commanding *Astrolabe*, proceeded to the village of Asu, several miles to the west. La Perouse was welcomed by the people of Fagasā village and permitted to fill his water casks from two streams which ran through the village. He strolled about the village, visited several Samoan *fales*, and was much impressed by the wealth of the society as represented by food stuffs and game fowl. The only things that detracted from his visit to what he characterized as a South Sea paradise were evidence of battle wounds on his Samoan hosts and a scuffle which developed between a native and a sailor engaged in filling the water casks. The native had struck the sailor with a mallet, and in retaliation the boat crew threw him into the water.

DeLangle did not take his men ashore for water until the next day. The passage through the reef at Asu appeared to be a dangerous one to negotiate. Therefore two deep draft barges were anchored outside the reef and two shallower draft longboats were taken ashore. Once on the beach the crew began filling their water casks from a fresh water stream while about two hundred Samoan spectators watched their progress. When the crowd suddenly grew in size to over a thousand, the Frenchmen began to be alarmed. DeLangle noticed that several men whom he perceived to be chiefs were attempting to maintain order over a crowd that was showing signs of becoming unruly. These men were given a few blue trade beads, but this only angered the others. At this point the mob began to stone the French sailors. DeLangle was among the first hit, and when he fell he was promptly clubbed to death. The survivors of this first volley of stones attempted to launch the longboats, but since it was low tide they could not be floated. The men abandoned the boats and waded out to the edge of the reef where they had moored the two barges.

DeLangle and twelve of his crew lay dead on the beach or on the reef flat, victims of what some believe to have been retaliation for the punishment of the Samoan involved in the scuffle with one of La Perouse's men at Fagasā on the preceding day. The Samoan villagers claimed that those who precipitated the massacre were not local people at all but a visiting party from the island of Upolu. A monument to the dead sailors still stands in the village of Asu, and on modern charts their cove is labelled "Massacre Bay."

Strangely enough, the Samoans paddled their outrigger canoes out to the French ship the next day and attempted to trade as though nothing had happened. This, and the fact that the French dead were buried with honors and their graves preserved, may indeed substantiate the claims that those responsible for the deaths were foreign visitors and not Asu inhabitants at all.

Captain Edward Edwards visited Samoa in 1790 while engaged in his search for the Bounty mutineers. His ship, *HMS Pandora*, lay off the island of Tutuila for a short period of time for purposes of trading. The Samoans, who traded foodstuffs for iron tools, proved to be so friendly that Edwards had great difficulty getting them to leave his ship as he prepared to leave.

MISSIONARY ACTIVITY

The first missionaries to arrive in Samoa were the Wesleyans in 1828. The mission's commitment to the area, however, was token, consisting of two native teachers from Tonga. Seven years later more teachers arrived under the leadership of Reverend Peter Turner, and a permanent mission settlement was established on the tiny island of Manono. Although the Wesleyans were the first to arrive, they were soon challenged in their race for converts by proselytizers of the London Missionary Society. The first LMS station in Polynesia had been established in Tahiti in 1797 with the sanction of King Pomare. From here the LMS extended its operations westward, arriving in Samoa in 1830. In that year the head of the LMS mission effort in the Pacific, John Williams, called at Upolu in the brigantine *Messenger of Peace* and left two native teachers to begin organizing a local church. The first European missionaries arrived in 1836, and at this time formal mission stations were set up on Tutuila and in the Manu'a group under the leadership of Archibald Murray and George Lundie.

Although missions were established by the Roman Catholics in 1845, by the Mormons in 1888, and in recent years by Seventh Day Adventists, Nazarenes, and a variety of Pentecostal churches, the major religious influence in Samoa over the years has come from the London Missionary Society, now known as the Congregational Christian Church of Samoa. Beginning with their project of reducing the Samoan language into writing in 1834, the London Missionary Society workers have had a profound impact both religiously and educationally upon Samoan lives. Although most Samoans are still familiar with ancient mythology and perpetuate some aspects of traditional spirit lore, nearly one hundred percent of modern Samoans would identify as both Christian and literate.

THE WILKES EXPEDITION

The first American explorer to call at the Samoan islands was Commodore Charles Wilkes while in command of six ships on a survey mission known as the United States Exploring Expedition. Wilkes has been recognized by American scholars as a competent man of science, and although there is evidence that he was something less than an ideal naval commander, he produced an excellent six-volume report of his enterprise which documents local customs, languages, and physical characteristics of native peoples on scores of South Pacific islands. The orders for what has become known as the "Wilkes Expedition" directed the Commodore to explore and survey the South Pacific Ocean in the interests of American commerce and whaling and "to extend the bounds of science, and promote the acquisition of knowledge." His expedition was specifically directed to visit the Society, Samoan, Fiji, and Hawaiian Islands.

The Wilkes Expedition arrived in the Samoan archipelago in October of 1839 and spent five weeks surveying the entire group. Wilkes' first introduction to Samoan islanders came on the island of Ta'u (which he erroneously referred to as Manua), where he arrived just in time to discourage a war between Christian converts and the "devil's men." He anchored off the northeast coast of Ta'u and went ashore at a village which his account indicates to have been Faleasao. Here, he and his party were immediately surrounded by Samoans wanting to trade for fishhooks and tobacco. Wilkes found the Manu'an people to be "a finely-formed race, . . . lively and well-disposed, though in a wilder state than those of the Society Islands." He pronounced them "not altogether honest," for in their trading transactions they were inclined toward "selling their articles twice over; for after we had made a purchase from one, another would claim the articles as belonging to himself, and insist on also receiving a price for it."[2]

In a tour of what we may assume was Faleasao village Wilkes observed thick stone walls which he presumed to be fortifications (although they could have been enclosures for pigs), chief's houses on raised stone terraces, and large outrigger canoes "capable of containing twenty or twenty-five men, and . . . very swift."

There is no evidence that Wilkes visited the village of Fitiuta, although his survey boats took soundings around the entire island of Ta'u. The expedition stopped at Ofu and Olosega, and Wilkes states that at the latter of these islands he met the Tuimanu'a (king of Manu'a) who was temporarily living in Olosega instead of his usual residence in Ta'u out of fear for his life. The king claimed that two warring factions—the Christians and the "devil's men"—had made his self-imposed exile necessary. After eating with the king and participating in a kava ceremony (where Wilkes refused kava in favor of the liquid of a fresh coconut), the Commodore experienced difficulty in attempting to leave the island. The king and several other chiefs climbed into the ship's longboat and refused to leave until they were given gifts of fishhooks.

After surveying the Manu'a Group, the Wilkes Expedition moved on to Tutuila, Upolu, and Savai'i. While at Upolu, Wilkes appointed John C. Williams consul to represent American interests in Samoa and to work with local chiefs in guaranteeing protection for the American whaling fleet. Williams was the son of the London Missionary Society worker who was responsible for the establishment of the Samoan mission in 1830. Actually his appointment as consul was never confirmed by the American government, although he was officially named to the post of commercial agent for the United States some five years later.

---

[2] It is very likely his accusations of dishonesty resulted from a lack of understanding of the communal nature of family property.

COLONIAL POWER STRUGGLE

America had commercial interests in all of the Samoan islands during the mid-nineteenth century but so did Germany and Britain. A lively trade in coconut oil began about 1842, and while the United States participated in this commercial venture, its main interests centered around the harbor at Pago Pago which was felt to have potential as both a commercial depot and as a coaling station for commercial steamships and United States naval vessels.

In 1872, the *USS Narragansett*, under the command of Commander Richard W. Meade, anchored in Pago Pago harbor under orders to make some sort of treaty with the chiefs of Tutuila which would give the United States the exclusive right to build and maintain a naval base on the shores of Pago Pago Bay. In return, the people of Tutuila would receive "the friendship and protection of the great government of the United States."

The chiefs of Tutuila, headed by High Chief Mauga, convened and negotiated a treaty with Commander Meade on February 14, 1872. It established a set of commercial regulations for the port of Pago Pago and named a port authority board consisting of High Chief Mauga, the agent of the California and Australian Steamship Company, and the consuls of the major powers with interests in Samoa. The treaty was never given official congressional sanction, but the document did represent the first formal working agreement between the Samoans and the United States.

As far as the major powers—the United States, Germany, and Great Britain—were concerned, the real struggle for control of Samoa was going on in Apia. There, each of these Western giants maintained consuls and commercial agents, and these officials were constantly involving themselves and their countries in political intrigues. Each supported one or another of the several warring native factions competing for dominance of the Samoan chain. The struggle between two of these factions—the Malietoa line and the Tamasese line—became so intense that by 1889 the United States and Great Britain (backing King Malietoa) were on the brink of war with Germany which had thrown its support behind King Tamasese.

On March 16, 1889, seven warships—three German, three American, and one British—rode at anchor in Apia, ready to provide military support for the actions of their respective consuls. But none of these warships ever fired a shot in their nation's struggle for control of Samoa, for before the day was over, all but one—*HMS Calliope*—lay wrecked on the Apia reef, victims of a great hurricane which suddenly swept down upon them, taking the lives of 146 sailors. Believing the tragedy to be providential punishment, the three Western powers sent representatives to a meeting in Berlin on April 29, 1889, where a treaty was negotiated recognizing Samoa's independence under King Malietoa and restricting Western control solely to the town of Apia. This treaty maintained a shaky peace until December 1899, when the Western powers again came together and signed a convention which decreed that the Samoan islands be divided between Germany and the United States, with 171 degrees west longitude as the dividing line. Thus the islands of Savai'i, Upolu, Apolima, and Manono became a German colony, and Tutuila, Aunu'u and the Manu'a Group became an American territory. Britain withdrew all claims to Samoa but gained political rights in other South Sea areas such as Tonga and the Solomons.

Even before the final three-power settlement, the United States had moved ahead with their plans for a naval base on the island of Tutuila. They had, up to this time, undertaken no construction, however, and the Pago Pago Bay coaling station consisted only of a huge pile of coal laying out in the open, the run-off of which discolored the bay every time it rained. Ships taking on fuel tied up to buoys in the bay and the coal was ferried out by lighter.

In April 1899 Commander B. F. Tilley, commanding the USS *Aberenda*, delivered a cargo of coal and structural steel to Pago Pago. He then sailed for Auckland, New Zealand to obtain more materials, but returned in four months to assume the role of the first commanding officer of the naval station now under construction. When completed, the new installation would include a steel dock, a corrugated iron coal shed, a storehouse, a residence for the man in charge of the coal depot, and a fresh water reservoir.

THE AMERICAN NAVY IN SAMOA

The three-power convention of December 1899 imposed greater responsibility on the United States Navy than was originally envisioned. The Americans had hoped for an independent Samoa, but they now found themselves charged with the protection and development of five inhabited Samoan islands. In February 1900 President William McKinley turned over the control of all islands ceded to the United States to the Navy. It now became the duty of Commander B. F. Tilley to negotiate a Deed of Cession with the ruling chiefs of both Tutuila and Manu'a. The Tutuila chiefs, under the leadership of High Chief Mauga of the village of Pago Pago, were exceedingly cooperative and a Deed of Cession was signed with them on April 2, 1900. Negotiations with the people of Manu'a, however, were not as successful. In March of 1900 Commander Tilley travelled to Manu'a and went directly to the island of Ta'u, the seat of King Tuimanu'a Eliasara. He landed at Ta'u village and was taken to the ceremonial guest house of the king, a middle-aged man who was a graduate of the London Missionary Society college, Malua, in Upolu. Tuimanu'a Eliasara was quick to inform the naval commander that the Manu'a Group was politically independent of Tutuila, that they had never played any part in the power struggle between the European powers, and that they did not want to align themselves with any faction now. The king stated that the Manu'ans would acknowledge the United States' sovereignty and would accept its protection, but he vehemently refused to cede his islands to the United States as the chiefs of Tutuila had done.

This stalemate continued until 1903 when Commander E. B. Underwood, a newly appointed commandant of the Pago Pago naval base, visited Manu'a and was confronted with a complaint by the Manu'an king concerning the poor quality of education in the Manu'a islands. The Tuimanu'a informed Underwood that the London Missionary Society school was no longer operative and that there were four or five hundred children who needed some kind of formal education. The king thereupon presented Underwood with a letter addressed to the President of the United States requesting a school, a teacher, and the necessary educational materials. Seeing a chance to use this issue as a bargaining point in extracting a Deed of Cession, Underwood promised that one hundred dollars a year would be provided for a new school, that Eliasara would be named District Governor of the Manu'a District, and that the Manu'a chiefs who would sign a Deed of Cession would receive recognition and gifts equal to those given to the chiefs who had signed the Tutuila Deed of Cession. The king and the paramount chiefs of Manu'a accepted these terms and on June 14, 1904, Manu'a was officially incorporated into the territorial holdings of the United States.

AMERICAN INFLUENCE IN MANU'A

Governmental control over the Manu'a Group has never been oppressive. Generally the Navy kept well within their initial agreement that:

> The customs of the Samoans not in conflict with the laws of the United States concerning American Samoa shall be preserved. The village, county, and district councils consisting of the hereditary chiefs and their talking chiefs shall retain their own form or forms of meeting together to discuss affairs of the village, county or district according to their own Samoan custom.

When the United States Department of Interior took over the governance of the Samoan islands from the Navy in 1951, the above policy was continued and is honored today.

No other portion of the Samoan archipelago is more isolated than the islands of the Manu'a Group. There are no docks nor harbor facilities at any of the villages, and contact with Pago Pago or with the other villages on Ofu and Olosega is possible only by way of an interisland motor vessel which touches at the various villages approximately once a week. In the not too distant past this vessel visited Manu'a but once a month. Until recently, when American teachers have been stationed on Ta'u, there were no permanent white residents. Two Navy pharmacist mates were assigned to the Manu'a area during the Navy's administration and there have been occasional Mormon missionaries living in Fitiuta, but generally white visitors have been of a very transient variety—government doctors, school supervisors, or economic experts—on short trips of inspection for the Government of American Samoa.

Western medicine is represented in the Manu'a Group by the presence of a Samoan medical practitioner who maintains a dispensary in Ta'u village and by trained Samoan nurses who hold daily sick call hours in Fitiuta. Foreign goods and foodstuffs are sold in Fitiuta in small family-operated stores, most of which have limited inventories and remain in business for but short periods of time because of poor management and lack of sufficient capital and access to an adequate flow of goods.

Because of its relative isolation and its strong, conservative local government— dominated by middle-aged and elderly *matai*—Fitiuta has remained one of the least acculturated villages in the Samoan archipelago. Manu'a offers no permanent commercial or public works employment opportunities, and young men who seek employment in activities other than subsistence agriculture or modest cash cropping enterprises must leave the village and take up residence on Tutuila or in the United States.

2 / The world of the *fale* and the *fono*

In Fitiuta, as in all parts of the Samoan archipelago, the important units of social organization are the household (*fua'ifale*), the extended family (*aiga*), and the village (*nu'u*). There are some sixty-five households in Fitiuta with an average size of nine to ten people. In charge of each household is a titled male, known as a *matai*, and this individual (sometimes referred to as "father") is responsible for the behavior and for the welfare of all who live under his authority. Each household maintains a village plot of land on which are located several sleeping houses (*fale o'o*) with elliptical floor plans and a large round guest house (*fale tele*). To the rear of these buildings there is usually a simply constructed cook house (*faleumu*) and frequently a privy (*fale'ese* or *falevao*).

Those who live with the *matai* usually include his immediate family (spouse and offspring) plus an assortment of collateral relatives such as elderly parents, grandchildren, aunts and uncles, brothers and sisters of the *matai*, and their families. The group may also include people who have been formally or informally adopted by the household head. The largest household in Fitiuta numbers twenty-two persons. Household composition is, however, somewhat impermanent because Samoans have a wide choice of households in which they may live, and mobility from one household to another is a common feature of Samoan family life. People are normally welcome in any household with which they have blood or affinal ties.

The head of each household holds the chiefly title of a given extended family (*aiga*) or branch thereof, and, depending upon the traditional nature of that title, will be either a Chief (*ali'i*) or a Talking Chief (*tulafale*). The nature and status of a given title is largely dependent upon mythological or legendary traditions. A Chief may be recognized as being of paramount rank, for example, because it is commonly recognized that the initial holder of the title was a direct descendant of the Tagaloa family of gods. A very high Talking Chief title may derive its status from the acknowledged fact that legends report that the original title-holder rendered exceptional service as an orator for a king or represented his village well in some historic negotiation with other villages or with other island kingdoms. Lesser titles have been created by the village council of chiefs as rewards to men who have served their community well, and sometimes powerful families have been able to prevail upon the village elders to allow them to create secondary family titles for men who were exceptionally capable but who would not ordinarily have a chance to attain chiefly rank until the family title-holder died.

Titles are conferred upon men for life through election by the members of the extended family, and the title is considered just as much the property of the family as are the lands and other forms of material property associated with it. Every Samoan *aiga* has, in effect, a home village where its elected *matai* resides and where its village and agricultural land is located. Only a portion of the *aiga* lives with the *matai* on these lands, but they are responsible to the larger group for the general maintenance of the status of the title and the welfare of the property.

Since Samoans claim membership in a given *aiga* by virtue of blood, marriage, or adoption ties to the original or subsequent title-holders, all Samoan *aiga* are large, and any given Samoan can always trace a relationship to, and therefore membership in, a dozen or more *aiga*. Because personal status can be derived from being related to important families, Samoans pay a great deal of attention to genealogical matters. It is a poor Samoan indeed who cannot claim at least one king or paramount chief as a relative. Needless to say, *aiga* with important titles tend to be large and *aiga* with recently established or lower ranking titles contain but few individuals.

Normally the *aiga* tends to be invisible. That is to say, it becomes a viable entity only when the *matai* dies and it must select a successor, or when it is called upon to contribute goods to the *matai* when he must represent the family in a gift exchange at the time of a funeral or wedding or when a large church donation is required for the construction of a new village house of worship.

Some insight into the approximate size of an *aiga* with a high-status title may be gained from court records of succession disputes which required adjudication because the family could not settle the issue themselves. In one such case a panel of one American and two Samoan judges attempted to settle the dispute by having members of the several family factions present petitions with the signatures of those supporting the various candidates for the *matai* post. The total number of names of people claiming *aiga* membership, and therefore eligibility to vote for one candidate or another, amounted to 961, or approximately one thirtieth of the total population of American Samoa. Actually, some of the names appearing on the petitions were residents of Western Samoa.

The several family factions referred to above in this Fitiuta title court case were actually separate branches of the family and were what Samoans refer to as the *faletama* (houses of the children). The phenomenon of *faletama* may be explained as follows: Let us say that the original title holder in a particular family had two sons and a daughter. This would mean that for all time to come this family would be recognized as being composed of two male branches and one female. Theoretically, the male branches are more eligible for title succession and therefore special privileges are provided the members of the female branch, known collectively as the *tamasā* (sacred child) or *ilāmutu* (sister's children). The relationship which exists between the male and the female branches of a family is called *feagaiga*, and as Milner (1966:83) defines it, it involves a pledge on the part of the male branches "to pay respect, to render services, and to observe certain obligations towards those descendants" in the female branch or branches.

It has been said that the female branch has the power of veto over decisions of the family, but in reality any family difference would rarely go that far, since Samoans believe that to ignore the wishes of the *tamasā* faction would result in family misfortune and even sickness or death of family members.

This general pattern of deference to the female side of the family is also reflected in the patterns of daily face-to-face interaction between siblings and other relatives of the same generation who are of the opposite sex. Samoans have a classificatory system of kinship terminology and therefore cousins as well as siblings must adhere to a set of norms which has commonly been labeled "brother-sister avoidance." Relatives who stand in this real or fictive relationship must not use language that is salacious or even suggestive in one another's presence, they must not remain alone together in a house, dance on the same dance floor, and generally not give any impression of affection for one another or in any way be suspected of any degree of intimacy whatsoever. Such rigid restrictions, while relating to incest prohibitions, no doubt also serve as a constant reminder of the more general obligations of deference which one owes the female side of the family.

When a family title has been vacated because of the death of its holder, members of the various branches of the *aiga* come together to deliberate concerning a possible successor. Often each of the *faletama* has its own candidate for the post, and deliberations are frequently long and painful. Some students of Samoan culture have maintained that in the selection of a successor there is a tendency toward primogeniture, and some have suggested that there is a special "right of the brother" to the position. Examination of several dozen genealogies through several generations revealed, however, that while it is common for a son to succeed to his father's title, there was no evidence of a "right of the brother" to the vacant title.

Men are elected to hold titles on the basis of their service to the family, individual intelligence and initiative, knowledge of ceremonial protocol, age (a *matai* younger than forty is an oddity), and in recent years, amount of formal education, wealth, and ability to deal effectively with Europeans in economic or political affairs. If the son of a deceased *matai* meets the criteria for family leadership, he will have a strong chance of acquiring his father's title, but this is a matter of family service rather than direct kinship ties. A young man who lives in the household of the *matai* and takes an active part in its day-to-day operations has a decided advantage over someone who, although also a kinsman with close blood ties, has been residing in another household. Qualification for title succession can involve a good deal of gamesmanship. For example, a young man who wishes to become a *matai* might very well see it to his advantage to take up residence with an uncle who has no male children of his own. Potential for title succession may also be a factor in marital residence. It is often a better investment for the future for a young man to move in with his wife's people where there is no viable successor for the family title than to live in his own household where he may be a second or third son and therefore have formidable competitors in his efforts to make notable contributions to the family welfare. In recent years some rather faithful and hardworking young men have been greatly disappointed when they have been bypassed as title successors in favor of other male relatives who have been absent from the household for several years attending school or working in the United States but who return when they hear that their family *matai* title is vacant. Families are often unduly impressed by stateside experience and feel that people with such a background can enhance the status of the family.

Family deliberations in the choice of a new *matai* may go on for several days or even weeks. Meetings are usually presided over by a *matai* who is related to the family, and everyone over about sixteen years of age has his or her chance to comment on the qualities of the men under consideration. It may be pointed out that one's favorite candidate is "familiar with the legends and myths of Samoa," or that he is "a man well respected by the other *matai* of the village," or that he is "a man of wisdom who can help the village in matters of agriculture and livestock raising."

Candidates do not speak in their own behalf, but are well represented by their supporting kinsmen. When a family has at last come to an agreement on a given individual, a kava ceremony involving only the family will be held to honor the new *matai*. He will drink first kava (the premier position) and later will be the honored guest at a family feast. In addition to the preparation of food and kava, it is also the family's responsibility to send a representative to the village council of chiefs to officially inform them of its choice. The village council will then set a date for the *fono tau a'a ti*, the official ceremony of title installation. On the appointed day the new *matai* will enter the council meeting, sit at the house post reserved for his title, drink kava in the order of his new rank, and then will be expected to deliver a speech, known traditionally as the *a'a ti*. This is, so to speak, the *matai's* first test within the village council. In it he is expected to show his wisdom and his grasp of oratorical protocol and expertise in turning a phrase or alluding to a mythological or legendary event appropriate to the occasion. It is said that in old Samoa if the chiefs found this speech lacking in quality they would refuse to recognize his right to sit in council. There is no such practice today. After the new *matai* has had his say, his fellow chiefs will also give speeches in the order of their rank, each imparting a bit of advice to the novice.

The newly elected family head now faces a second test by the village—his ability and willingness to provide food in generous quantities for village feasting. Not only must the new *matai* and his family provide food for all families, but each of the *matai* in the council expects substantial gifts such as finemats or money. These gifts are presented to the chiefs by a titled relative of the newly installed chief. This distribution of property, called *mālō toga*, will be accompanied by pronouncements such as, "This is the time we give you finemats for the new *matai*." The council is then dismissed and the newly installed chief returns to his family to begin his new lifetime role as family head and "father" to his household.

While *matai* are theoretically selected to serve for life, there are exceptions. Occasionally an irresponsible, lazy, or cruel chief may have his title removed by his family in a kind of impeachment action, or it may be that a very elderly chief will find the responsibilities of his role beyond his abilities and will voluntarily remove himself as *matai* so that a younger, more energetic man may take over and therefore find reward for years of faithful service to the family.

ROLE OF THE *MATAI*

Once elected to head the family, the *matai's* responsibilities are manifold. He serves as a kind of family patriarch who must promote family unity and prestige, administer all family lands, settle disputes among kinsmen, promote religious participation, and represent the family as its political spokesman in the village council of chiefs (*fono*). The *matai* must even strive to take on a new personality, for once he is a chief, he becomes a man of increased importance, a man of responsibility. Something of the nature of the role may be gleaned from the following statement of a young chief recorded by Margaret Mead:

> I have been a chief only four years and look, my hair is grey, although in Samoa grey hair comes very slowly . . . But always, I must act as if I were old. I must walk gravely and with measured step. I may not dance except upon most solemn occasions, neither may I play games with the young men. Old men of sixty are my companions and watch my every word, lest I make a mistake. Thirty-one people live in my household. For them I must plan, I must find them food and clothing, settle their disputes, arrange their marriages. There is no one in my whole family who dares to scold me or even to address me familiarly by my first name. It is hard to be so young and yet be a chief (1928: 36–37).

All land in and around Fitiuta which is not designated as "village land" belongs to one or another of the extended families who have *matai* in the village. Private ownership of land is almost nonexistent. The *matai* is said to have *pule* over the land of his family. This means that he has the power to determine the uses to which family land is to be put, that is, what portions are to be cultivated and for what crops. While a *matai* may lend land to friends or relatives who do not live within the household unit to be used in growing certain short-term cultigens, he does not have the authority to alienate family lands through sale or gifts. Any such transaction which would result in permanent loss of *aiga* property must be entered into by all members of the extended family, and a unanimous decision must be reached. Such an agreement is difficult to obtain, for Samoans are extremely reticent to be separated from landholdings. The Government of American Samoa supports this sentiment by stipulating that no one without seventy-five percent Samoan ancestry may purchase land.

Most Fitiuta families work their lands as a family unit, moving from section to section as a single work force. Village members often combine their efforts in working for community projects which will benefit the whole, but in normal subsistence agriculture or in cash cropping there is little cooperative labor outside the family circle.

The fruits of family labor are theoretically shared equally among all the members of the household, regardless of how much or how little labor each has actually contributed. The *matai* is responsible for making an equitable distribution, but he is also expected to accumulate wealth which can be used by the family in times of economic crisis or to meet their social obligations. Such obligations might be gift presentations at a kinsman's wedding or funeral or special church donations.

In modern Samoa the communal nature of family property and labor is beginning to break down. More and more, young men are demanding an opportunity to earn money of their own. In a place like Pago Pago this is not a problem, for a young man can obtain a job with the government, in some aspect of the tourist trade or in one of the commercial establishments such as the fish cannery, but in Fitiuta private enterprise requires the cooperation of the *matai*, since agriculture on family lands is the only available source of cash income. There has always been an opportunity for young men to go high on the mountain slope, clear bush land, harvest a crop, and sell it for personal gain, but today there is an increasing pressure on *matai* to divide up family lands and allow heads of nuclear families within the household to work them as private enterprises. Such changes in the economic operation of the family have not, however, impaired the position of the *matai* in the family and village structure. Young men now have the opportunity to manage their own money, but the obligations due their family and their *matai* remain the same. A recent survey revealed that sixty-six percent of the families of Fitiuta permitted untitled members to work "private" land, but in spite of this, every *matai* in the village claimed that he received generous donations from the members of his household to promote family prestige and well being. Since every untitled man looks forward to someday being elected to a title, and since gifts to the *matai* and to the family as a whole are considered a form of service (an important consideration in the selection of a *matai*), there is still a great deal of income-sharing within household units. In spite of the greater emphasis now being placed on the individual in the economic and social interactions of the household, the average Samoan is still committed to the traditional system. Even among teachers and government office workers in Tutuila (the most acculturated of Samoans), it was found that better than three-fourths believed that the *matai* system is adequate for shaping the future of Samoan society.

Even though individual family members often cultivate "private" plots, much of the family agricultural work is still a joint family enterprise under the direction of the *matai*. In most cases the *matai* works beside the members of his family expecting no special privileges. There are times when the *matai* must attend the village council meetings, but generally he contributes as much physical labor as any member of his group.

To assist the *matai* in the planning and execution of family labor activities, he will select an assistant who is commonly referred to as the *matai taule'ale'a*. This is an untitled man, often the chief's son, who serves as labor foreman and takes over the *matai*'s duties when the latter is away from the village or involved in council deliberations. Every morning the *matai taule'ale'a* is expected to go to the family head and discuss the work plans for the day. Together they may decide, for example, that half a dozen young men and women should spend the morning weeding in the taro patch on the upper slope, while two young men should remain behind to repair the thatch on the sleeping houses or perhaps do the family cooking for the day. Still other family members may be assigned to fish or search for small octopuses or shellfish on the reef flat.

There has been a good deal of lack of understanding among foreign observers concerning the power and authority of the *matai* and the *taule'ale'a* to make demands on the labor of household members. Some have believed that the *matai* has an almost life and death control over his family and that these poor individuals have little choice but to obey the dictates of their autocratic leader. As Fay Ala'ilima writes in her book *A Samoan Family*:

> The *matai* might give his *taulele'a*[1] orders but he was also obliged to train them and to see they were happy. The village *fono* made him pay the fine when his *taulele'a* got into trouble. His *taulele'a* came to him with their personal needs and *fa'alavelaves* (troubles). The whole village would laugh at him if his *taulele'a* became dissatisfied and left. A *taule'ale'a* might not talk back directly to his *matai* but he had other ways of expressing himself. Pai had yet to see a Samoan feel or act like a slave. The very thought made him smile (1961:29).

Actually, the Samoan household group is run very democratically. With the freedom that Samoans have concerning choice of residence (for example, they are always welcome for any period of time in the home of any kinsman), no *matai* can really force anyone to work for him unless he wants to. One informant confided that when he was a child he would always change households just prior to the time when he knew he was about to be assigned a particularly disagreeable task. Young people and adults, however, usually take the bitter with the sweet, and unless their *matai* is particularly authoritarian and unreasonable, they are quite willing to abide by his decisions for the sake of an efficient and prosperous household. *Matai* of high traditional rank tend to be more demanding of their people because they realize that being associated with a household of a high-ranking chief is prestigious, and there is less chance that people will seek residence elsewhere, even though they might find certain demands oppressive.

Much of the agricultural work is demanding in strength. Land may have to be cleared with axes and bush knives, and very heavy loads of produce must frequently be carried long distances over rough terrain, but normally hours spent in agricultural work are not long. The average family can provide itself with ample food for a week with only six to eight hours total labor in a seven day period. Additional time may be spent keeping houses or pig fences in repair or in fishing on the reef, but no Samoan has ever experienced the oppressive situation of the American

[1] *taulele'a* is the plural form of *taule'ale'a*.

or European's eight-hour day. Normally Samoans farm in the cool of the morning, nap in the heat of the day, fish when the tide is right, and care for their buildings when they require attention. They work with speed and enormous energy to complete a difficult task, and when they are finished they feel no guilt in sitting around idle and unproductive. The Western man's concept of "keeping busy," whether there is a worthwhile or necessary task to be completed or not, is foreign to the Samoan's value system. In tasks which Samoans and Europeans would find equally important, the latter would be hard put to compete either in terms of expenditure of energy or in dedication.

CHIEFS AND TALKING CHIEFS

All *matai* titles may be categorized as being that of Chief (*ali'i*) or Talking Chief (*tulafale*—one who sits in the front of the house). Within the Chief category the uppermost station is that of the *ali'i sili*, or High Chief. Such individuals often hold paramount rank in a village or may share top honors by being part of a group of "brother chiefs" who have great influence in village affairs. *Ali'i sili* titles are always very old and usually have a great deal of traditional lore associated with them. A holder of such a title is usually quick to relate that his title, for example, was originally awarded to an ancestor for extraordinary bravery in battle or for wise and faithful counsel to a Manu'an king. One Fitiuta *ali'i sili*, Galea'i, documents the high status of his family title with myths (recorded by Williamson and Churchill) that the Tagaloa family came down from heaven and bestowed the *ao* (crown) title upon a newly born Manu'an boy named Galea'i who thereupon became the first chief of all Manu'a. *Ali'i sili* titles were awarded to families as dowry or as gifts by important personages in elaborate gift exchanges with distinguished and deserving subjects. When High Chiefs take their reserved seats (identified in terms of house posts) in the village council house for meetings of the *fono*, they are located at the ends of the elliptical floor plan.

Next in order of importance within the Chief category are the *ali'i* (Chiefs) who are also heads of extended families or of branches of families but who do not have titles of sufficient traditional status or authority to warrant special attention in the power structure of the village. In village council meetings (*fono*) they sit on the flanks of the *ali'i sili* at the ends of the house.

The lowest rung within the Chief category is occupied by the *ali'i fa'avaipou* (between the posts Chiefs). These men are also *matai* but usually of branches of large families. Their titles are often of relatively recent creation and they are usually younger men who perhaps will later be selected for more prestigious titles. They often sit near the Chief who holds the paramount title in their family and usually side with him in village decisions. As the term for these Chiefs indicates, they frequently do not have assigned posts where they may regularly sit in council meetings but must often resort to sitting cross-legged on the mat near the senior Chief of their family. It is quite likely that most of these titles were specially created long after the original village hierarchy was established and the accompanying seating plan for the village council formalized.

Talking Chiefs may also be described as occupying three levels of importance. Of highest rank is the *to'oto'o*, or *tulafale sili*. These men are often orator chiefs for High Chiefs and usually serve as spokesmen for the entire village in intervillage ceremonies or negotiations. Their posts in the *fono* seating arrangement are at the front and the back of the council house. They are flanked by Talking Chiefs of secondary rank known in Fitiuta as *vae o to'oto'o* (feet or legs of the Talking Chief). Next to them, and sometimes without permanent post assignments, are the lowest rank of Talking Chiefs, the *lautī laulelei*, or *tulafale fa'avaipou* (common, or between the posts Talking Chiefs).

It is difficult to generalize concerning the functions of the various grades of Talking Chiefs when we consider Samoa as a whole, for each village tends to have its own structural peculiarities. Buck states, however, that

> there are grades of prestige among the Talking Chiefs depending, no doubt on the political influence held by the family from which they derive their titles. The higher grades of Talking Chiefs are naturally those historically associated with ruling high titles. Where the lesser *tulafale* represented their family groups, the higher ranks represent the village which is a combination of families (1931: 72).

Some observers of the Samoan political scene give the impression that Chiefs and Talking Chiefs come in pairs, that is, every Chief has a Talking Chief who does his speaking. This is generally true in the *fono*, but not necessarily in individual families. There are cases where the senior title in a family is a High Chief title and a lesser title is a Talking Chief title. In such cases the orator chief will speak for his Chief, making his wishes known much as a lawyer speaks for his client. Chiefs may, however, and often do, speak for themselves in village council meetings. The paramount title in some families is of the Talking Chief variety, and its holder is therefore obligated to express his family's wishes himself. In the *fono* he may speak not only for himself, but he may be historically linked to another family headed by a High Chief and this, of course, increases his oratorical responsibilities since he may have to speak for both families.

ROLES OF CHIEFS AND TALKING CHIEFS

The role of Chief varies with his rank within the village hierarchy. In some villages there is but one individual known as *ali'i sili* (High Chief), while in others there may be a group of "brother chiefs" who hold *ali'i sili* rank. High Chiefs preside over the village council, help settle disputes which arise there, and serve as advisors to the Talking Chiefs. Such an individual is a village leader and maintains a great guest house for the entertainment of important visitors to the village. In many cases he traditionally has had the right to appoint his daughter or a close relative to the position of village ceremonial maiden (*taupou*), and his son was qualified to serve as the leader or *manaia* of the village society of untitled men, the *aumaga*.

A High Chief's rank permits him to drink first at kava ceremonies and he is entitled to the first portion (*sua*) of food when chiefs eat together. When large amounts of food are distributed at feasts or at gift exchanges, his portion always consists of the most desirable portions of the pig, fish, or fowl. A High Chief's share of a pig, for example, is the loin. Some *ali'i sili* have the right to impose *tapu*, which amounts to declaring the reef off limits for fishing for a period of time prior to a community fishing drive (*lau*), or forbidding anyone to harvest taro prior to a great feast. Some insight into the traditional role and status of the High Chief may be gained from the fact that they are collectively known as *fa'atui* (second to the king).

The roles of second- or third-rank Chiefs differ very little from one another. Being of lesser rank, they do not have the responsibility of giving their opinions in village council deliberations. They may, however, contribute to decision-making discussions, and some of these men exhibit great wisdom and analytical ability on such occasions. If the High Chief is absent from the council meeting, a Chief of secondary rank will occupy his post and preside over the meeting after the fashion of a vice-president in an American club or business meeting. While High Chiefs are permitted to carry a large and bulky fly whisk as a symbol of office, Chiefs of secondary rank carry only a small whisk which is more appropriate for shooing flies than signifying rank. Secondary Chiefs must be very careful that their symbols of office do not compete with those of the higher ranks, or they may be accused of "assuming above their rank." In times of high ceremony High Chiefs are expected to wear tapa cloth wrap-arounds, but lesser Chiefs are not expected to appear so formally or ceremonially garbed.

The *tulafale* are undoubtedly the most colorful of titled men, particularly the High Talking Chiefs, who occasionally are identified as "the difficult people" because of their ability to persuade, cajole, or intimidate through their artistry with words and protocol.

Samoan tradition explains the division of titles into Chief and Talking Chief categories by citing the *mavaega* (last will and testament) of the culture hero Pili, who divided the islands of Upolu and Manono among three of his four sons, but gave the fourth the fly whisk and the right to speak for the Chiefs of the family. Regardless of whether such an event ever occurred, the fact remains that Talking Chiefs have special advantages over Chiefs, as well as special opportunities for gaining wealth and public acclaim. Buck comments that specialization of chiefly functions

> reached its highest in Samoa where a class of hereditary talking chiefs termed *tulafale* created such a mass of observances in etiquette, precedence, and a special chiefs' language, that the high chiefs were unable to do without them.

Talking Chief with orator's staff.

No high chief could travel to other villages without his official *tulafale*. Not only did the talking chiefs create increased ceremonial around the high chiefs, but they became administrative chiefs with regard to the distribution of food and presents and thus acquired a great deal of power previously exercised by their superiors (1965:166).

As with Chiefs, there are various levels of Talking Chiefs. The High Talking Chief, who has the traditional right to carry an enormous *fue* (fly whisk) serves as principal village orator, settling disputes between villages, welcoming important persons or delegations (*malaga*) upon their arrival in the village, directing and announcing important kava ceremonies, and overseeing distributions of food and other property when events involving the entire village take place. His skill at persuasion is often so great that few individuals except High Chiefs dare oppose him. In village council meetings it might be said that he organizes the agenda and is often responsible for placing motions before the assembly.

In addition to his key role in the village council, the High Talking Chief is closely associated with the phenomenon of the *malaga*. A *malaga* is an official party of titled individuals who journey to another village or island for the purpose of carrying out some practical or ceremonial function. There is, for example, the *malaga tapa fala* (the visit to ask for mat-making materials), the *malaga ta'aloga* (the visit to engage in competitive sports), the *malaga si'i* (the visit to exchange property associated with a marriage), and many others. In every case the visiting party must be accompanied by a High Talking Chief, and the party must in turn be welcomed, feted, entertained, and ceremonially bid goodbye by the High Talking Chief of the host village. Each of these aspects of a ceremonial call presents a major occasion at which orator chiefs may demonstrate their rhetorical ability—flattering the guests and bringing honor to themselves and the village as masters of protocol and as perfect hosts.

Oratory is a fine art among these men, and there are highly prescribed procedures which must be followed and elaborate structures for speeches which must be committed to memory. Most important of all is the knowledge they must have of *fa'alupega*, the official list of names and relative ranks of a village's Chiefs and Talking Chiefs and the appropriate esoteric and symbolic references which relate to the social and political structure of the village. Since 1946 *tulafale* have had some help in acquiring this information, for on this date the London Missionary Society Press published a book containing the *fa'alupega* of all the villages in the Samoan archipelago. The Talking Chief of a *malaga* arriving in Fitiuta, for example, would have to include in his remarks to the host village the following recitation of Fitiuta village organizational characteristics:

Tulou na Fitiuta.
(Hail to all the Chiefs and Talking Chiefs of Fitiuta.)
Tulou na le faleula tau aitu.
(Hail to the red house of spirits—the *fono* of Fitiuta.)
Tulou na le Tamaa'ita'i o le Ao.
(Hail to the Lady of the Dawn—symbolic reference to the title of High Chief
  Galea'i.)
Tulou na le Vaimagalo. O le susu mai le Pulefano.
(Hail to Galea'i and Soatoa, ambassadors to the court of the King of Manu'a.)
Tulou na lau afioga Tufele.
(Hail to High Chief Tufele.)
Tulou na Faleifā ma Ma'opū o le Alofiamoa.
(Hail to the four houses of Chiefs and the Ma'opū division of Chiefs.)
Mamalu maia fetalaiga ia te outou To'oto'o.
(Hail to the Speakers, the High Talking Chiefs.)
Tulou na le Suafa o Nu'u.
(Hail to the rulers of the village.)
Tulou na le So'oso'o Ali'i ma le Taua'ese'ese.
(Hail to all Chiefs and Talking Chiefs of secondary rank.)
Tulou na le aumaga paia le i fafō.
(Hail to the sacred society of untitled men seated outside the council house.)
Tulou na le alofi e magalo ai mea uma.
(Hail to the kava ceremony which cleanses everything.)

Once past the elaborate courtesy phrases the orator is free to use his imagination and creative skill. The bodies of speeches are always ornate—filled with obscure references to mythology and amply supplied with Biblical phrases and allusions. In its ceremonial context, oratory functions less as communication than as art.

Children's dance group entertaining visiting malaga.

Great orators have a hundred and one devices for holding attention or highlighting important statements or ideas. Generally the voice volume rises from a whisper to nearly a shout as the speech proceeds. Now and again a special point will be emphasized with a gesture of the fly whisk or a sudden clipped phrase. A momentary pause or a sudden reduction of voice volume highlights a thought of which the orator wants his audience to make special note. When interest appears to lag, a bit of sarcasm or humor or a proverbial cliche may be used to renew flagging attention spans. As in all Samoan social interaction, the phenomenon of reciprocity is evident in oratory. It is a gracious institution which honors and flatters others but also brings great satisfaction, prestige, and community admiration to the artful practitioner.

The Talking Chiefs are also the poets of this society, being responsible at the time of kava preparation or as a part of a speech for a recitation or even the composition of verse known as the *solo*. *Solo* often feature rhyming couplets and predictable meter patterns and usually deal with mythological or legendary subject matter and undoubtedly owe much of their form to the age-old chants of Polynesia. While *solo* lose a great deal in translation (particularly their rhyme and meter) and often deal with mythological events which have little meaning for those outside the culture, these poems hold a measure of appeal even for the foreign reader.

Solo ia Afoafouvale

Sleep, I sleep deeply;
I awaken.
Did I dream, did I call out in my sleep?
Did I anoint myself with oil?
Did I dye my hair with the juice of the puni leaf?
Did I sleep in the company of noble women?
What is the confusion of men's and women's voices?
Is there a distribution of finemats?
Is there feasting?
Has the sacred fish of the sea arrived for the feasting?

While the greater share of ceremonial glory goes to the High Talking Chiefs, second- and third-rank Talking Chiefs also play important roles. Their fly whisks do not match those of first-rank orators in size nor do their occasions for speech-making match those of the High Talking Chiefs in importance, but there is still an ample portion of prestige to be enjoyed. They have adequate opportunities to speak in the decision-making deliberations in village council, and it is here that they develop their skills to be used in other ceremonial contexts. Many *malaga* arrive with only an orator of secondary rank, and this gives the host village orators of equivalent rank an opportunity to perform. The Samoan sense of fair play eliminates the possibility of their matching the skills of a High Talking Chief with those of a lesser-ranked orator in the exchange of speeches which mark the initial stages of intervillage interactions.

Talking Chiefs of secondary rank also serve as messengers to other villages and often represent the interests of their extended families in disputes and deliberations with other *aiga* within the village or in other villages. The Talking Chiefs are generally thought of as the masters of ceremony on any occasion. It is the importance of the occasion which determines the appropriate rank of the one who will officiate.

THE *AUMAGA*

The untitled men of the village are known as *taule'ale'a* and represent the main labor force in both the household and the village units. At the village level the untitled men (often referred to as "young men" regardless of age) are organized into a cooperative work group called the *aumaga*. This unit has both labor and ceremonial functions and serves the village council and the village as a whole. Sometimes referred to as "the strength of the village," this associational group assists the chiefs in ceremonial activities and carries the bulk of responsibility and effort in all village cooperative enterprises. They plan and provide the bulk of the labor force in such activities as cutting copra for church money-raising projects, repairing village paths, housebuilding, ferrying passengers and cargo in longboats to vessels anchored outside the reef, planting and harvesting of the village taro patch, and group fishing (*lau*) on the reef flat.

For the village council, the *aumaga* cooks and serves food at all *fono* meetings and on all ceremonial occasions. They have the prime responsibility in the wringing and serving of kava. They also serve as a kind of police force, enforcing all village council legal pronouncements.

The *aumaga* is an entirely voluntary association made up of the untitled men of all the households in the village. The leader of the group is called the *manaia* which literally translated means "a fine looking man." In his ceremonial and leadership roles he serves as a kind of village "prince" since he is the "son" of the paramount Chief. While this young man may not be an offspring of the paramount Chief, he is always a relative whom the chief refers to as *atali'i* (son), and this may also include grandsons, brothers' and sisters sons', and even adopted sons.

When the *manaia* convenes his group, the result is a junior version of the village council. The *manaia* presides as his father does in the village council, and the sons of Talking Chiefs carry out oratorical functions not unlike their fathers. *Aumaga* decision-making procedures are much the same as those followed in the *fono*, and in the actual carrying out of work projects the chain of authority mirrors that of the hierarchy of chiefs. One significant difference between this group and the senior elite group is that the *aumaga* also serves its members' recreational needs. The *aumaga* members often come together for cricket playing or to play cards far into the night. They aid one another in courtship activities and they often rehearse and perform group dances (*sasa siva*) to entertain visiting *malaga* or in dance competitions at church dedications or Flag Day celebrations. Occasionally the group will get together for a beer party much to the disapproval of the village chiefs.

THE *AUALUMA*

The female counterpart of the *aumaga* is the *aualuma*. It is an organization of unmarried women with representatives from the several household family groups which make up the village. Their function, like the *aumaga*, is to contribute to the general welfare of the village through a variety of social, economic, and ceremonial activities. But while the *aumaga* has remained relatively unchanged in its structure and function over the years, the *aualuma* has changed drastically. Originally the *aualuma* was a group of handpicked unmarried women who served the village ceremonial virgin princess, the *taupou*, as handmaidens and chaperons. They were constantly in attendance, sleeping with the young woman and caring for all of her needs. The *taupou*, who stood in the same relationship to the paramount Chief as the *manaia*, that is, a real or fictive daughter, was the center of ceremonial attention and in most villages was the principal kava preparer and dance leader. She represented the "cream" of the village young women and her virtue was carefully protected in anticipation of a "noble" marriage with an important chief or *manaia* from another village. At the time of her marriage the *taupou* had to submit to a public defloration ceremony in which the village High Talking Chief inserted his finger into her vagina (wrapped with snow white bark cloth) and hopefully obtained the scarlet evidence of her purity.

There is still a group of young women in every village today who are known as the *aualuma*, but the traditional *taupou* institution has passed. There are no permanent ceremonial virgins today and therefore no need for the *aualuma* as originally constituted. *Taupous* are appointed by paramount Chiefs from the ranks of female relatives for specific occasions, like the entertainment of a group of official visitors (*malaga*), but these young women are often married women with children—obviously not virgins.

Today the *aualuma* serves a very different function. Composed exclusively of unmarried girls and widows, it is but a part of a greater village organization known as the Women's Committee which also includes wives of untitled men and the wives of Chiefs and Talking Chiefs. While still a recognizable entity, the *aualuma* works closely with the other women of the committee in public health and infant welfare activities, in raising money for the village church, and in the entertainment of *malaga*. It is characteristic of the group to come together and weave mats or house blinds for the pastor's residence or the dispensary or even to produce them for sale to raise money for village enterprises. The Samoan medical practitioner has come to depend on these ladies for promotion of the weekly baby clinic and for the extras in dispensary equipment and supplies which the government does not provide.

The *aualuma* serves much like the *aumaga* in that it undertakes much of the heavier work which middle-aged and elderly chief's wives are incapable of doing. They are particularly singled out for such activities as group dancing, an indispensable feature of every Flag Day celebration. Since the girls in this group average in age between thirteen and twenty-one, they are the logical candidates for the strenuous and exacting demands associated with this art form. On ceremonial occasions such as this they appear with their appointed *taupou* in specially prepared costumes and go through the painstakingly learned series of unison body movements which comprise the *sasa siva*. The *aualuma* also occasionally carries out special work projects of its own initiation apart from the Women's Committee. Under the direction of an elderly widow they often plan and undertake collective shellfish forages on the reef flat or meet together to make tapa cloth which will serve as valuable exchange property for some future *malaga* encounter or as a village gift at some future church dedication celebration in a distant village.

The principal leadership of the Women's Committee comes from the wives of High Chiefs and High Talking Chiefs who rule the organization by virture of their husband's positions in the village hierarchy. Their official meetings are not unlike those of the *fono* in form or function, as the pattern of decision-making is almost identical in this group as in that of their spouses.

(Top) Aualuma *dance group doing a* sasa siva. *(Bottom)* Aualuma *dance group and dance leader at village celebration.*

A DAY OF DECISION

The first hints of midday heat were appearing as the *matai* of Fitiuta began to assemble in the village council house. The sun was high and the low overhang of the thatched roof provided ample shade for most of the posts where the chiefs settled themselves, ready for a prolonged period of discussion and debate in the *fono faleula tau aitu*. Many of the older chiefs had already laid out their bundles of coconut fiber and had begun braiding them into stout sennit. The men talked softly and lit up large "cigarettes" of locally grown tobacco rolled in dry banana leaves. There was some discussion of the topics that would be debated during what promised to be a long day. The most important decision that would have to be made concerned what would be done about the reconstruction of the village guest house which was destroyed in a recent storm. The roof had been blown off and there was damage to the center posts and to those that supported the superstructure around its oval floor plan. The house clearly had to be rebuilt from top to bottom. But such an undertaking was beyond the abilities of anyone in the village at the present time. While there was an excellent group of carpenters in Fitiuta, they were presently engaged in a project in another village and would not return for several months. Today the *fono* would have to decide on a course of action. Should they wait until their own carpenters returned and possibly suffer the loss of prestige for not being able to quarter guests in a house of great quality and size, or should they summon carpenters from another village and have the work begin immediately? If the latter course were followed they would have to decide where the village would get the money for a down payment, for the carpenters' food throughout the time of construction, and for a final payment upon completion.

La'apui and other high ranking village orators had already discussed the problem informally in a meeting known as a *taupulega*, which is a kind of caucus wherein some consensus is sought prior to the formal *fono* discussion. This informal discussion had explored the issues but had not settled them. It had assessed support for, or opposition to, the matters to be debated. Such meetings are considered important, because Samoan chiefs are wary of putting full support behind projects in which they cannot count on some aid from their fellow chiefs. Finally the Talking Chiefs had set a date to bring the matter before the *fono*. Today was the day. They had taken the responsibility of passing the word well in advance so that each of the *matai* would have ample time to discuss the issues with his family and crystallize his opinion.

When all the Chiefs and Talking Chiefs had arrived in the council house and the *aumaga* had taken its position in two tight rows outside, the council members were welcomed and thanked for attending by the *to'oto'o*, La'apui, the orator who would preside over today's gathering. Although the chiefs and their untitled aids were all present, and all in attendance were anxious to get to the issues that had brought them together, there were formalities which must take place before any debate could begin. In Fitiuta and in every village in the Samoan chain the kava

A member of the society of untitled men (aumaga) *prepares the kava root for the bowl.*

ceremony is invariably the initial act of any meeting of the village council. After the kava has been mixed and served to each *matai* in order of his rank, it would be time to begin the business at hand. The kava ceremony would, in a way, insure that success would be achieved in the subsequent deliberations.

The kava ceremony began with La'apui selecting a kava root from the many that had been laid out before him on the mat. The appropriate root was then handed to a member of the *aumaga* who cut it into pieces ceremonially referred to as "scales of the sacred fish." The "sacred fish" reference alludes to the fact that kava, like many *tapu* foods, is the exclusive property of the elite ranks. The pieces of kava were then pounded into pulp, the consistency required for proper steeping. While the kava was being pounded on the concave surface of a rock, other *aumaga* members washed the multilegged wooden kava bowl and brought clusters of coconut-shell containers filled with cool, fresh water.

While these preparations were being made, an air of reverence prevailed within the council house. Chiefs spoke only in whispers and no one smoked. At a location near the back of the house three members of the *aumaga* positioned the great wooden kava bowl and sat down cross-legged behind it. A fourth man stationed himself outside the house, ready to carry out his function as strainer cleanser. The village *manaia* sat directly behind the bowl. He would prepare the potion. The man to his right emptied a leaf full of pulverized kava root into the bowl and filled the bowl half full of water. The man to the left of the *manaia* sat patiently and with dignity. In time he would serve the finished product to the assembled chiefs. The youth about to prepare the drink wore nothing above the waist, and his *lavalava* was turned up so that it would not extend below the knees.

The role of the *manaia* in this ceremony is a highly prescribed one permitting little innovation or departure from established procedure. Almost without thinking he went through the traditional motions of steeping the kava. First he covered the kava in the bottom of the bowl with a fibrous strainer made of hibiscus bark. Then he pressed down on the strainer with the heels of his hands. Pulling his hands toward him, he collected the kava pulp and lifted the strainer high above the bowl. Then with a motion not unlike that used to grip the handle of a baseball bat, he wrung the strainer three times. He bent his hands forward so the kava would not run down his arms and waited for the last of the golden liquid to cascade into the bowl. Then he repeated the entire process two more times. Now with a sweeping motion of the arm he threw the pulp-filled strainer backwards out of the house where it was skillfully snared by the strainer cleanser who removed the kava pulp with several snaps of the fibrous bark strainer. It was then

The manaia *wrings kava for the assembled village council* (fono).

thrown back into the house and the *manaia* repeated his earlier steeping procedures. Each time the kava fell into the bowl from the wringing, the *manaia* observed its color and the sound of its splashing. This would tell him when the potion was right for drinking. When he judged that this was the case, the *manaia* wiped the rim of the bowl, cleansed the strainer by snapping it himself, and then dipped the strainer into the bowl one final time and raised it so a generous stream of kava showered down into the bowl. This gesture, known as the *sila alofi*, permitted the chiefs to judge if the kava required more water. Observing that it didn't, La'apui began the ceremony by singing out in a high-pitched voice: *"Ua usi le alofi"* (The kava is already cleansed). In response to this announcement the assembled chiefs clapped their hands, not as applause, but for protocol.

La'apui now began to announce who should be served using, in many cases, cup titles rather than *matai* names. Cup titles are poetic or honorific phrases which draw upon mythological allusions and not infrequently mention sacred events, persons, or places. The cup title of one of Fitiuta's High Chiefs is "The Dawn at Saua which is the supreme authority." This refers to the creation morning in the Samoan Garden of Eden. Only Chiefs of considerable status have cup titles. Talking Chiefs receive their cup after only the words *"Lau 'ava"* (Your kava), and Chiefs of secondary rank with the invitation *"Taumafa"* (Drink).

The order in which the *matai* receive their kava is of vital social importance. The Chief of highest traditional rank drinks first; then the highest ranking Talking Chief. The cup is then passed to the second ranking Chief, the second ranking Talking Chief, and so on down the elite hierarchy. In some villages, groups of chiefs drink before other groups, thereby placing somewhat less emphasis on the individual's unique social position. Regardless of the procedure, the greatest prestige is associated with being the first to drink, and strangely enough, the last to drink. In Samoa, the cliche "last but not least" has been made an institution.

Now the bowl was empty and La'apui announced *"Ua moto le alofi"* (The kava is finished). *"Ale le fau ma le ipu e tautau"* (The bowl will hang with the strainer and the cup). Having concluded the necessary ceremonial commitments, the council now turned to the business at hand, mainly the question of the construction of the guest *fale*.

The opening speech was made by a High Chief of the *Ma'opū* division of the Fitiuta council. It was noncommital and expository in nature and represented an attempt to clarify the issue without taking a definite stand. The other members of the council recognized the speech as a deliberate attempt to feel out public opinion on the matter.

The second speech came from a Talking Chief of low rank speaking for his High Chief, a member of the *Faleifā* branch of the council. The speech resembled the one preceding it, although it further clarified the issue at hand and spelled out the alternatives. While the speech contributed little, it represented an opportunity for a young chief to display his wisdom and oratorical skills.

Next to speak was a low ranking Talking Chief from the family of Ve'e, a

High Talking Chief of the *Suafanu'u* group of orators. He was not speaking for the senior chief of his family, but merely expressing his own opinion. He felt that the village should wait for its own carpenters to return and not go to the expense of importing builders who would be, after all, strangers. This opinion was seconded in a speech by another lesser ranking Talking Chief of the family of the presiding officer of the *fono*.

High Chief Ale then entered a contrary opinion—that they must soon have a guest house or they would be embarrassed when *malaga* arrived and they had no place to entertain them. If it meant that they had to bring in carpenters, then so be it. High Talking Chief Ve'e agreed with Ale, thus expressing an opinion contrary to that of the junior Talking Chief of his family. Then High Chief Nūnū spoke in favor of importing carpenters as soon as possible, and High Chief Paopao stated his agreement. Thus the position of the village elite was known. They wanted to build a guest house as soon as possible. Opposing them had been only two lesser ranking Talking Chiefs. La'apui, the presiding officer of the *fono*, sensed that a majority opinion had been established and, hearing no further arguments in opposition, stated that the village would contact a head carpenter from another village (probably on Tutuila) so that the work could start as soon as possible. Ways of financing the enterprise would be discussed at a future meeting.

The decision was considered by the chiefs to be a unanimous one. If there had been further opposition to the position of Ale, Ve'e, Nūnū, and Paopao there would have been an attempt to reach a compromise resolution, but in this case the opposition disappeared when the majority opinion became apparent. A Samoan majority is not calculated in numerical terms, for the opinions of the higher titles carry more weight than those of lower ranking *matai*. Even if half a dozen lower ranking chiefs had opposed the opinion of the four high ranking members, the verdict would have been the same. Every *matai*, regardless of rank, has the right to speak, and if his arguments are convincing he may very well influence how the men of high rank vote. There are no raised hands, "aye" or "nay" responses, and no ballots. Speeches represent votes, and the presiding chief must assess the mood of the council from their oral pronouncements. Samoans believe that decisions should be reached only after a period of spirited discussion, but if that discussion is going their way, chiefs will refrain from speaking since silence is interpreted as approval of the general point of view dominating the debate. *Fono* meetings are often long because council members believe that the more important the issue, the longer it should be deliberated.

Many decisions are reversed at a later date, providing the dissenters can marshal sufficient support, for Samoans believe that decisions should never be inexorable. Although the opinions of men of high rank carry great weight, there is a genuine attempt in all discussions to arrive at a solution which will be agreeable to all council members regardless of rank. Samoan decision-makers realize that only those decisions which are seen as group products are effective in promoting council and village harmony and solidarity.

3 / The world of work

In Fitiuta every man can build his own house, fashion a canoe (*paopao*) out of a breadfruit log, plant and harvest a field, and bring home an adequate meal for his household after an afternoon of reef fishing with a hook and line or a throwing net. While a great deal of knowledge of the world of work is shared among the 492 members of Fitiuta village, there is also an easily recognizable division of labor between the men and women, the young and old, and the ordinary worker and the specialist.

Tufuga in Samoa means "specialist" or "expert" and should not be confused with the use of the term in eastern or central Polynesia where it essentially refers to a religious specialist, a priest, but also may be used for experts in other fields. In Samoa a *tufuga* may be an expert tattooer, boat builder, house builder, or surgeon (in the case of circumcision), but the term is not used to designate a religious specialist or an expert fisherman.

Most work is a cooperative affair and people toil together in family groups, in special association units such as the *aualuma*, the *aumaga*, or the Women's Committee, or in a group involving the total village. Fruits of men's and women's labors are shared freely without regard to the relative input of individuals. The industrious and lazy alike enjoy adequate food, clothing, and shelter, but there is pride and prestige for those who do their share and more. For the young untitled male, efficient and conscientious labor is a way of distinguishing himself as a promising candidate for some future family *matai* title.

Samoans are mainly subsistence agriculturalists, devoting only a fraction of their time to exploiting the resources of the sea. Most cultivable land is associated with one *matai* title or another, but there is some bush land—technically the property of the village—which is available to individuals with enough motivation and energy to clear it and keep it under cultivation.

The *matai* is said to have *pule* over the family lands. This essentially means that he has administrative control. He has the power to determine the uses to which family lands are put, but this control does not allow him to negotiate any transaction which will permanently alienate the land. This can only be done with the unanimous consent of the extended family. The *matai* does however have the authority to loan fallow lands for the growing of short-term crops to neighbors or family members living outside the household. While modern practice permits the *matai* to allocate portions of family land for personal use and profit, all family lands remain the property of the extended family. When the *matai* dies, the *pule* passes to his successor. It is not possible for a *matai* to will sections of land to his offspring, even though they may have been farming them on an individual basis for a considerable period of time. The only case in which the rights to a given section of family land may be acquired by an individual is in the case of a *tofi*, which is a gift of land made with total family consent to a member of the family who has made some outstanding contribution to the group's welfare.

The pattern of land ownership and utilization remains much the same today as it has for centuries and involves the following categories: (1) village house lots, (2) plantation plots, (3) family reserve sections, and (4) village land.

Village house lots are those grassy sections of village land on which the household dwellings stand. This cluster usually consists of a guest house, sleeping houses, and assorted out-buildings. Graves of deceased relatives are found here, and in some cases a section has been set aside for a small taro patch. There may be a few breadfruit, papaya, or coconut trees on the lot, but generally village sites are not considered appropriate for agriculture.

Plantation plots are found along coastal areas outside the village limits and on the lower slopes of hills rising above the community site. Coastal plots are considered best for coconut groves, and slopes are favored for breadfruit trees and banana plants. Every family has a number of "plantation" plots (usually not contiguous) in various locations outside the village. Rights to plantation lands are clearly defined and everyone is aware of the natural features (rocks, particular trees, streams) which are used in determining exact boundaries. Most plantation land is grown up with underbrush, and agriculturally important trees and plants are not planted in orderly rows. It is quite possible that one who is not familiar with South Sea island flora could walk right through a plantation without realizing that it is under cultivation. Some taro is found in this area, but more frequently the main taro patches are located higher on the slopes in what might be called family reserve sections.

Family reserve sections are also the property of village families and have well recognized boundaries, but they are used less intensively than the plantation plots. These sections are normally planted in more quickly maturing crops such as taro, yams, and bananas, and this land is more frequently loaned to friends or neighbors for the growing of a single crop or two, but is rarely loaned on a long-term basis. Samoans find no difficulty in differentiating between land ownership and crop ownership. In many cases land will belong to one family and the crop growing on it will belong to another. In such cases the land owners have no claim to any of the produce unless they have been specifically given that right by the cultivator. The fact that one's family owns the land does not alter the fact that to take food that has been planted by someone who is using the land on loan is still theft.

Village land lies even farther up the mountain slopes than family reserve lands and is used only occasionally by villagers, and only then with the express permis-

Husking coconuts—an initial stage in copra production.

sion of the village council. An individual with energy enough to clear this densely covered bush land has claim to the land as long as he continues to cultivate it, but once his plot is taken over by underbrush he loses claim. These lands may also be used by any of the villagers for wild pig or pigeon hunting.

Village land includes not only bush land high on the mountains, but it also includes reef and sea frontages which may be used at any time by individuals for angling or net fishing (unless the area has been temporarily *tapued* by the village council) or by the total village, or by a component organization, such as the *aualuma* or *aumaga*, for large-scale fish drives (*lau*).

AGRICULTURE

Both men and women engage in agricultural work, although generally it can be said that men do the strenuous work, such as land clearing and planting, while women weed and help in harvest activities. Both may be seen carrying unbelievably heavy loads of produce home from the plantations in woven coconut leaf baskets placed on the ends of a wooden carrying pole which serves as a yoke.

Land is cleared by the men using axes to fell the large trees and bushes and bush knives to remove the high grass, ferns, and other scrub vegetation. The plot is then left for a week or more so that the leaves will drop from the trees and the trunks and branches may more easily be cut up for burning. These sections of trees as well as brush are disposed of in controlled bonfires, but the land itself is never burned over.

The principal tool used in planting is the pointed hardwood digging stick (*oso*) which is two to four inches in diameter and between three and four feet long. This implement is used both to pry out rocks from the field and to break ground, the latter operation involving forcing the stick into the soil and then pulling it backward in the direction of the planter. Bits of tuber (in the case of taro, sweet potatoes, and yams) or young plants or suckers (in the case of bananas) are placed in the hollow made by the digging stick and the earth is packed down with the bare feet or hands. Once a banana grove is flourishing, there is little need for fresh planting. When harvested the stalk of the old plant is merely cut off close to the ground and the young suckers growing around its base are allowed to mature into another plant. In the case of breadfruit, new trees are started from saplings which are found growing wild in the bush and transplanted. Papaya trees are rarely planted but merely spring up from seeds discarded when the fruit is eaten by people working on plantation lands. Oranges and mangos are collected from trees growing wild in the bush, but some families purposely propagate them from seeds. Coconut trees, which supply Samoans with the major share of their cash income, are planted from whole nuts which are allowed to sprout and buried approximately two feet deep.

No terracing is done and no irrigation is practiced. Ditches may be dug to retain rainwater for wet taro beds, but for most crops the tropical rains which occur almost daily provide sufficient moisture. No special fertilizer is used although *gatae* trees (*Erythrina*) are planted on agricultural land so that their fallen leaves may decay and improve the quality of the soil.

Of all the products of Samoan agriculture the coconut is unquestionably the most useful. Besides being about the only product from which Fitiutans derive cash income (from copra), this tree provides a host of useful products. The strong, heavy wood is used for some house components, headrests, rollers for canoes, cricket bats, and fuel. The leaves are woven into baskets, house blinds, food trays, fans, hats, floor mats, sandals, toys, and units of thatch, although sugar cane thatch is preferred. Sennit, the cord used in all house lashings and outrigger lashings, is made from the fibers found in the outer husk. The meat, besides being dried and sold as copra, has numerous uses as a foodstuff. The raw kernel of the mature nut is often eaten as a snack by people working on the plantation or is taken along on bonito fishing expeditions as a source of nutriment. The meat of the green nut is especially prized when eaten raw or grated and used as a basic

Copra destined for Pago Pago being loaded into longboats for transport to a motor vessel anchored outside the reef.

ingredient in a number of dishes. Grated coconut when compressed in a strainer produces a whitish liquid known as "coconut cream," which is also a vital part of many Samoan recipes. Coconut shells provide Samoan cooks with many of their culinary utensils. They serve as water bottles, dishes, and food scrapers. Discs of coconut shell also provide the game pieces in a competition known as *lafoga*, which is played something like shuffleboard. Coconut shell is also used in the manufacture of hooks for bonito fishing.

The kernel of the mature nut when compressed in a strainer woven of hibiscus bark produces oil (*lolo*) which Samoans use for a variety of cosmetic and medical purposes. It is used to groom the hair, oil the skin (on ceremonial occasions), and since it is often scented with fragrant blossoms, it is used as perfume or cologne. Swimmers oil their bodies for warmth, and *lolo* is used as a dressing for cuts and sores. It is rubbed on the chest as a remedy for coughs and it is taken internally to relieve stomach aches or constipation. *Lolo* is, however, never used in foods or as an oil in pan or deep frying.

The cool, slightly sweet tasting water to be found in the immature nut is a refreshing drink, and to offer a guest a freshly opened drinking nut is often an initial gesture of welcome. When the coconut matures this liquid is replaced by a spongy white substance which serves as a basic food for pigs as well as an occasional snack for humans.

While the coconut is the Samoan's most valuable all-around agricultural product, their favorite foodstuff is taro. The starchy grey tuber of this plant is prepared by either boiling or baking but it is usually eaten cold. It is never mashed into *poi* as is the practice in eastern Polynesia. Bananas, prepared by boiling or baking and also eaten cold, are also a preferred foodstuff. In most cases the fruit is used while still in a green state and it is rare when Samoans allow the fruit to ripen. While the people do occasionally just peel and eat a yellow banana, fruit in this state of ripeness is usually pulverized and mixed with other ingredients in dishes like puddings or fruit drinks.

While less preferred than others, the food which seems to find its way to the Samoan food tray more frequently than any other is breadfruit. During the three breadfruit bearing seasons the trees produce fruit in such abundance that much of it falls to the ground, rots, and produces a terrible stench. Breadfruit is often buried in the ground in what the people refer to as *masi* pits as insurance against possible future crop failure or other natural disaster. When these storage pits are uncovered, often many years later, the breadfruit will have decomposed into a foul smelling mass not unlike very old cheese. It will be cut out in chunks, wrapped in leaves, and baked. It is considered a great delicacy. When prepared fresh, breadfruit is usually baked, but there are a number of recipes which utilize pulverized breadfruit in the form of dumplings.

Everyone in Samoan society is first and foremost an agriculturalist. Even traditional specialists, like tattooers, housebuilders, canoe builders, and master fishermen spend part of their time on their agricultural lands. There are no agricultural experts, although some people are recognized as being more successful than others. It is everybody's job, male and female, child and adult; the assigned tasks are merely different for those in different age and sex categories.

Many Manu'a villages attempt to establish a weekly work schedule so that there will be some coordination of effort within the community. These are formulations resulting from village council deliberation. Fitiuta has such a plan and it involves the following scheduling:

Monday—All untitled men and their *matais*, along with the younger and stronger women, work their own land, clearing, planting, or harvesting. Only fuel and subsistence foods may be brought back to the village. One product which must not be harvested is bananas. That is done on Tuesday. Nor can cash crops (copra in particular) be harvested.

Tuesday—Family work groups cut bananas for household use for Tuesday, Wednesday, and Thursday, and other subsistence foods may be harvested. Copra can be cut with the permission of the village council.

Wednesday—Rhinoceros beetle searching is carried on between 6 A.M. and noon. Plantation work, or repair work on houses, pig fences, or village paths is appropriate for the afternoon. Wednesday is often a copra-cutting day.

Thursday—Necessary chores are accomplished as designated by family *matai*. Village regulations do not specify appropriate nature of work.

Friday—Bananas are harvested for family use for Friday, Saturday, Sunday, and Monday. Cooking for weekend needs is begun in the evening.

Saturday—A cooking and fishing day. Little or no agriculture is carried on. Since meals are more elaborate on Sunday, fish are obtained in order to add variety to the normally vegetable diet. Because Sunday is a day of rest, food preparation is carried out on this day.

Work plans are formulated with a definite rationale in mind. They are not merely arbitrary creations of chiefs who want to wield power. Since some people have more coconut trees than others, village council regulation is a means of making sure that there is some control over theft. If all families work their groves on a given day, there is less opportunity for thieves to go unobserved. On other days thieves bringing copra back from the bush can easily be spotted because this is not the appropriate product for the day. Limiting the harvest of bananas to Tuesday and Friday is also done to control theft. Although Sunday is designated as a day of rest and families are forbidden to even prepare food, Sunday does not officially start until daybreak, and many cooks rise early and carry out their food preparation activities prior to dawn.

FISHING

There is a commonly held fallacy that Polynesians spend a great deal of their time fishing or gathering shellfish. This is not true, as the above work schedule will testify. While Samoans are extremely fond of fish and really prefer it to other forms of protein, they really spend very little time angling, spear- or net-fishing, or scavenging on the reef. Undoubtedly more time was spent in these activities in the past, but today it is often easier to send someone to the bush store for a tin of sardines, tuna, or salmon than to spend hours trying to catch fresh fish.

While fishing activities consume perhaps a tenth of the time and energy devoted to agriculture, Samoans have devised an impressive array of methods for exploiting their sea resources. Fitiutans fish singly or in groups for a variety of creatures ranging from reef worms to giant turtles and sharks. Individual methods include the use of three kinds of throwing nets for capturing a host of brilliantly colored reef fish; wooden traps for taking eels, lobsters, crayfish, and crabs; bamboo rods with lines outfitted with metal hooks and lures of stone or shell or live bait for catching sea bass or red snapper; nooses for snaring small eels when they have been partially lured out of their lairs in the coral by sticks with small fish secured to the end; three-pronged spears for impaling, or bush knives for slashing a variety of fish and sea creatures; poisons and dynamite for killing whole schools of fish within the fringe reef; and spear guns, resembling sling shots, made of wood and strips of innertube which launch long missiles made of heavy fencing wire. The latter device is used on the reef flat or by swimmers operating well offshore who tread water for hours collecting whole strings of fish which they wear like a belt.

Three man crews in twenty-seven foot outrigger canoes fish for bonito often well out of sight of land, and danger-loving shark fishermen in rowing boats stalk their prey with heavy rope nooses which they slip over the heads of the sharks, lured to the side of the boat with chunks of meat. Turtles are captured by men in boats who place large banana leaves on the water as shade for the animals. The men return later and pick up the leaves. If they are lucky they will find at least one turtle under the leaves and be able to wrestle it into the boat. Community fish drives (*lau*) are carried out on the reef flat by large numbers of men and women who drag long streamers (made of coconut fronds twisted about vines) through the water and drive schools of fish toward men who wait with gill nets and spears. In some cases a rock cairn is prepared beforehand so that the frightened fish, in seeking its shelter, are concentrated in one small area. Gill nets are placed around the cairn and as one man unpiles the rocks, others spear or shoot the fish with missiles launched from spear guns.

Reef scavenging is carried out almost entirely by the women. They probe the holes in the coral reef with sticks and occasionally are successful in locating small octopuses which they drag from their shelters and kill by biting or by beating the creature on a rock. Crabs, lobsters, crayfish, and squids are also objects of their search.

THE FISHING SPECIALIST

An expert fisherman in Samoa is not referred to as a *tufuga*, as are other experts, but rather as a *tautai*. The term is peculiar to bonito fishing, and this is the only variety of angling that recognizes specialists. Bonito fishing is done from a twenty-seven foot outrigger canoe known as a *va'aalo*. Men sitting in the bow and the waist are paddlers (and occasionally bailers), while the *tautai* sits in the stern. He is not only the fisherman but also the captain of the craft. While many families in the village have bonito boats, not all families have *tautai* to command them and must contract with a specialist to operate their boat and fish for them. December is considered the best month for bonito, but the boats also go out in all months except March, April, August, and September. Samoans actually recognize three bonito seasons. Bonito feed in schools, and lookouts watch for telltale disturbances on the surface or for flocks of birds which prey upon the small fish attempting to escape the bonito. Once a school is located the bonito boats attempt to position themselves in the center and stay there. While the paddlers maintain their position relative to the school, the *tauti* gives his full attention to his rod and line. A heavy fourteen foot bamboo pole is put in place in a special set of blocks so that it points directly astern and forms a forty-five degree angle with the surface of the water. This pole streams a heavy section of line just long enough to allow a white clamshell lure with an unbarbed tortoise shell hook to skip along on the water. When a fish bites, the *tautai* gives a sudden heave on the pole, pulling the bonito out of the water. The more expert *tautai* can jerk the pole in such a way that the fish flies free of the hook and lands in the canoe. Since the boat may lose its position within the school at any moment, removing the hook from the mouth of each fish consumes valuable time. A very successful *tautai* may land as many as seventy or eighty fish, and it is often necessary for some of the crew to swim along side the boat so there is room for the catch.

Bonito fishermen usually fish in fleets, and there is a great deal of ceremonialism connected with this activity. When the day's fishing is over, all the boats are expected to meet just outside the reef by order of a special chief who rules the fleet. At this meeting the chief of the fleet first offers up thanks to God for the success of the enterprise and then asks the *tautai* how many fish each has caught. Those who have caught many must share with those who have caught few, so that every boat arriving home will have an equal number. Then the chief selects as many fish as will be required to feed all the crews and these are divided and eaten raw. The first share in each boat goes to the *tautai*. After this ceremonial meal known as the *aleaga*, the boats come ashore individually. The families that own the boats meet the crews, divide up the catch, pay off the men in fish, and return to their homes with their newly acquired wealth. Families of crews as well as families of boat owners are forbidden to do any work while the fleet is out. They are expected to remain idle and "pray for the fishing." *Tautai* say they know when families do not observe this tradition, for the bonito constantly slip off the hook before they can be landed. Those who remain idle are collectively referred to as the "family of Tuiatua," Tuiatua being a kind of patron spirit of fishermen.

HOUSEHOLD TASKS

Cooking   The culinary arts are the special preserve of the men. Since the members of the *aumaga* have always been designated as the special servants of the chiefs, ceremonial cooking has, over the years, been their responsibility and has probably established men as the proper cooks of traditional foods. While it has been claimed by some that women may not touch ceremonial foods because they menstruate and are therefore considered unclean, it should be pointed out that the most sacred ceremonial element, *kava*, is, in most villages (although not in Fitiuta), prepared almost exclusively by the *taupou*, the village ceremonial virgin.

While the older, more traditional ideas concerning strict divisions of labor are fading away, there still seems to be a pattern of men serving as the chief preparers of food, even in the household. In Fitiuta today there is a tendency for men to cook the more traditional foods and for women to take over the preparation of the newer foreign foods. Things that come out of a can or a box (like cake mixes) have become the special concern of women, and they are the ones who have taken to pan and deep frying and to such modern devices as kerosene or white gas pressure stoves. The women have furthermore added to the list of feast foods which now include dishes like chop suey, goulash, potato salad, pie, and cake.

The most traditional method of cooking, and therefore that used almost exclusively by males, involves the earth oven, the *umu*, wherein a fire is built over a pile of cooking stones on a level or slightly hollowed out floor of a *fale umu* (cook house). The pit cooking methods found in such places as Tahiti or Hawaii are not practiced in Samoa. The first step in preparing the oven is stacking up and igniting kindling on top of a layer of fist-sized black rocks. When the fire is burning well, other stones are placed on top, and within thirty to forty minutes the fiery embers and bits of charcoal are removed from around the glowing stones with wooden tongs and the stones are spread out in a circle some three feet across. Now the food (green bananas, taro, breadfruit, and often fish in leaf wrappings) is placed toward the center of the circle of heated stones. Wooden tongs are again brought into use to lift stones from the outside of the ring and place them on top of the first layer of food. Then another layer of food is added and another layer of stones. Leaves are often placed between the stones and the food so that it will not become charred. Finally, a blanketing cover of large breadfruit and banana leaves completes the oven preparation, their function being to hold in the heat.

The completed oven is left to cook for approximately an hour and then is dismantled with the wooden tongs used to build it. The steaming food is placed in a basket woven from coconut fronds and taken into the guest or sleeping house and allowed to become cold before it will be served.

Another traditional method of food preparation uses a large carved wooden food bowl and the heated stones from the *umu*. In the preparation of the much desired *tafolo sami*, for example, sea water and coconut cream (a liquid pressed from grated young coconut meat) is placed in the bowl and brought to a boil by dropping in hot stones. Then golf-ball-sized spheres of mashed breadfruit are introduced into the mixture and allowed to cook until they acquire the consistency of dumplings. Arrowroot and papaya puddings are also prepared utilizing this general cooking method.

Of all the foods cooked in the Samoan oven, pigs have the most ceremonial importance. No feast or celebration would be complete without pork being part of the menu, and the calculation of the number of pigs cooked is a way of documenting the degree of importance of a ceremonial occasion. However, very little pork is eaten at the feast itself (partly because most of it is undercooked), but large slabs are taken home by each of the guests to be enjoyed by their families on the following day.

Pigs are strangled by laying them on their back and standing on a stick placed across their throat. The carcass is then dragged across the heated stones of the earth oven in order to singe off the hair and bristles. The abdomen is then cut open, the internal organs removed and wrapped in leaves to be cooked separately, and the hollow abdominal cavity is filled with papaya leaves, which supposedly flavor the meat and act as a tenderizer. The whole pig is then placed on the circle of heated cooking stones with the feet tucked under the carcass. After receiving a cover of leaves, and sometimes a layer of damp burlap bags, the pig is allowed to cook for approximately one hour. In this period of time the animal will become only partially cooked, but there are outside portions which are done— enough to eat at the feast—but the important thing is that the meat can easily be divided without falling apart. It is important that these divisions be accurately made, for there is a standardized system of distribution according to relative rank. In any ceremonial distribution a Talking Chief representing the host family or village will make the official presentation of the head to the *aumaga* (the cooks); the neck and foreleg to the Talking Chiefs; the shoulder to the Chiefs of secondary rank; the loin to the High Chief; the rump to the wives of the Chiefs and Talking Chiefs; and the wall of the abdomen to the village ceremonial maiden, the *taupou*. Similarly precise divisions are made of chicken, turtle, sharks, bonito, and various other large fish.

Barkcloth   While barkcloth making is not an art which requires highly specialized talents, it is a skill which is reserved for women, and tapa cloths, called *siapo* in Samoa, figure significantly in *toga*, which according to long-standing tradition is the property associated with the female side of the family. It is exchanged ceremonially for *oloa*, the property of the male side.

Aside from their value merely as property to be exchanged, barkcloths have a number of practical uses. *Siapo* is often given to Talking Chiefs as a token of appreciation for duties rendered to a Chief or a village council. The cloths, which usually measure approximately four feet by six feet, are valued as ceremonial clothing and are worn by titled persons as wrap-arounds or kilts. A more commonplace use is made of them by women who use them as wrappers when they go out of the house at night. Larger cloths are used to partition off a section of the house or to grace a chief's European-style bed as a bedspread.

Barkcloths are but one class of items in the general category of *toga* which also includes finemats, floor mats, and, in modern times, lengths of trade cloth. Finemats continue to retain their position as the most valuable of the *toga* items, and old finemats are carefully protected in family storage chests and passed from family to family as occasions for property exchange arise. Most owners know the history of ownership of the finemats, their age, and the occasions of importance when they were exchanged. A new finemat may have a monetary value of about twenty dollars, but a very old and venerable one may be worth several hundred. Few finemats are made these days, except by an occasional old woman who has several months to devote to the activity and who has sufficiently good eyesight to cope with the hundreds of slender strips of hibiscus bast which form its warp and woof.

Barkcloth, on the other hand, is produced in moderate quantities by the women of nearly every household. Village women are always careful to make sure that there is a sufficient number of paper mulberry bushes under cultivation at all times to insure a ready availability of materials for their periodic manufacturing sessions.

While the women are responsible for nearly all stages of barkcloth production, it is the men who carve the boards which are used in printing geometric designs on the snow white mulberry bast. These boards are made of hardwood, but in earlier times *siapo* tablets were made of pandanus leaves placed in such a manner that their midribs formed designs. The modern boards measure about one by three feet and perpetuate the same kind of geometrical designs as were found on the old leaf tablets. Thus design motifs tend toward diagonals, squares, diamonds, and only occasionally circles or petal figures. While Samoans find rich floral designs appealing in trade cloth, the boards rarely follow suit. Thus the early limitations imposed by materials have produced a design tradition from which Samoans do not readily depart, even though the use of carved boards offers no design restrictions.

Each household usually has but one board, and this means that all the cloths produced by that household will have the same printed design and can therefore be easily associated with its producer. Variety is introduced by way of secondary painting with darker pigments over select elements of the design, but barkcloths are not valued for their unique or original qualities anyway.

The process of *siapo* manufacture begins with the stripping of the bark from a section of mulberry branch about an inch in diameter. The outer bark is separated from the inner bast, and the latter is placed to soak in a container of water. Clam shells with carefully sharpened edges are then used to remove the green coloring matter and the coarser particles which cling to the bast. Next, the back of the shell is applied to the bast to smooth it and to make it wider. Several strips are then bundled together and beaten with a hardwood beater on a *toi*-wood log. This fuses the fibers and extends the cloth to the proper width. This process may be compared to felting. When the individual sheets attain a width of about twelve inches they are stretched out on the mat to dry, with stones weighting the edges.

When dry, sections of the bast are placed on the printing board (*upeti*) and a wad of barkcloth dipped in a dye, extracted from the bark of the *o'a* tree, is rubbed over the fiber, the pressure bringing out the design of the tablet underneath. As sections of the mulberry fiber are imprinted, they are folded over and another section is glued in place with a glutinous adhesive (arrowroot) and the printing process repeated.

Weaving The making of pandanus floor and sleeping mats is a life-long chore for Samoan women. Girls twelve years old and sometimes younger are introduced to the various stages of mat production. They learn to collect leaves of proper width and length, process them, and finally plait them into the mats which form the main items of household furnishings.

The pandanus leaves (*laufala*) used for floor mats are approximately six to eight feet long and about five inches wide. The midribs are removed and the leaves are laid in the sun for four or five days to dry and bleach. Since the leaves often develop longitudinal wrinkles during this process, they are wrapped around the hand to flatten them and then wound onto a large coil which the women refer to as a *masina* (moon). The two-inch-wide leaves are then split in half, thus producing the strips which are used in the actual plaiting. Mats are woven diagonally in a simple checkerboard pattern and measure six feet by two feet in finished form. Floor mats are not dyed or decorated in any way.

Sleeping mats differ from floor mats in that the former have narrower wefts and they are softer, due to the fact that the leaf strips are steamed prior to plaiting. Sleeping mats are often decorated on the edges with yarn fringe, and occasionally a portion of the pandanus wefts is dyed and worked into designs over the whole or a part of the mat.

Weaving sessions occur with some regularity in each household, but special mat-weaving bees are also organized by the Women's Committee or just by neighbors to produce a stockpile of mats for some special purpose like outfitting the dispensary or the pastor's *fale*. The weaving bee may, on the other hand, be organized for social purposes, that is, women enjoy getting together for work projects, believing that the work does not seem as difficult if they can share each other's company.

THE CARPENTER'S CRAFT

Myths relate that the first Samoan house was built by Tagaloa-Lagi in his heaven on top of the highest mountain on Ta'u island. The family of Tagaloa felt the need for such a shelter, for up to that time people lived only in caves or in the trees. At first they could not decide whether they wanted to build a house first or a boat. They settled on a boat but then realized that the trees overhead would provide insufficient protection from the sun and the rain. They finally solved this problem by deciding to build a house first and then build the boat inside the house. Bonito boats are to this day built inside houses.

First Tagaloa-Lagi had to decide what materials would be used to build his house. He resolved that he would build it out of people. So a group of people were instructed to form a circle, thus providing the posts. Others were directed to climb on their shoulders in order to form the parts of the roof. Tagaloa-Lagi saw that the shape was good but that the house needed more support. The god then brought three fish from the sea, the *Falala* (filefish), the *Fe'e* (octopus), and the *Lupota* (crevally), to serve as center posts. There was still a problem of support. A wise man of the village suggested that a shelf (*fata*) be added as well as a ridgepole, arched gable beams, and a cross beam above the center posts. Other people climbed up and formed these parts of the house. Tagaloa-Lagi saw that the house was now strong and well shaped but decided that the house should be made of wood rather than people. He called to all the people to come down and go out and find a kind of wood from which to make the house. Of all the varieties of wood they brought in, only the breadfruit was judged suitable. And so the first house was built of breadfruit wood, the material still preferred by contemporary carpenters. After the house was completed, Tagaloa-Lagi said he was too old to build any more houses. He chose various members of his family to carry on the housebuilding tradition, and he selected Sao to be the chief carpenter of Manu'a. To this day, the *tufuga* (specialists) who build are known ceremonially as Sao, and although carpenters do not have any sort of guild organization, all men in this trade are generically referred to as belonging to "the family of Sao."

The term Sao includes not only house builders but boat builders as well. Some carpenters specialize in houses and some in boats, but there are craftsmen capable of constructing houses, canoes, bonito boats, and rowing boats (*fa'atasi*). Many of the builders of rowing boats are young, having learned the techniques of European boat construction in school. Rowing boats are made from stock lumber using screws and nails as fasteners. Bonito boats, on the other hand, use hand hewn planks sewed together with sennit and caulked with breadfruit gum. Their construction usually requires the talents of the older, more traditionally oriented craftsmen.

To become a carpenter a young man will approach an established artisan and request an apprentice relationship. He need not be a relative of the carpenter, although most crews are made up of kinsmen. The young man will work with the carpenter and his crew of laborers until he feels competent to launch out on his own. If he can negotiate a building project with someone, the young man will collect a group of workers and he is in business. He has, it might be said, acquired the status of Sao.

THE SAMOAN *FALE*

Samoan houses consist of a floor of coral pebbles, a series of outer posts set in a circular or elliptical plan, and a beehive-shaped roof supported in large measure by three center posts. Houses often rest on elevated platforms, called *tia*, their height corresponding to the relative rank of the elite occupant. While *fales* are normally open on all sides, blinds (*pola*) woven from coconut fronds may be let down from under the eaves in the manner of venetian blinds in times of inclement weather or to provide protection from the sun.

The roof of the house is composed of three parts—two gables (*tala*) and a center section (*itu*). This superstructure is a maze of beams, rafters, purlins, and ribs all held together with hundreds of sennit lashings, many of which are decorative in nature. No nails or other modern fasteners are employed.

The thatch, which is put in place by the owner and his family rather than the carpenters, is made up in units composed of sugar cane leaves twisted about a three foot long wooden rod. Like other parts of the house, the thatch units are held in place with lashings of sennit.

The traditional mainstay of the carpenters' kit is the adze, armed today with a steel blade instead of the stone head of former times. Other modern elements in the housebuilding complex include Western tools like the plane, the hand saw, and the brace and bit, but the product produced by these differs little from those

Sleeping mats and bedding stored for the day on a shelf (fata) *which is a structural part of the house.*

built a century ago with cruder tools. Carpenters build without blueprints or plans, and measurements are made in terms of standards somewhat less than acceptable to Western carpenters. The units of measurement are the *gafa* (the span of the outstretched arms—roughly a fathom), the *vae fatafata* (the distance from the tip of the outstretched arm to the middle of the chest—half a *gafa*), the *vae luaga o le lima* (the distance from the tip of the fingers to the bend of the elbow—one fourth of a *gafa*), and finally the *aga* (the distance from the tip of the thumb to the tip of the index finger in maximum spread). The *aga* is the unit most frequently used, and a typical order from a carpenter to one of his helpers would be to bring a post twenty-six *aga* in length.

THE COMMISSION

When a *matai* wishes to have a new house constructed he will call the members of his extended family together and request that they contribute food and sometimes money for an initial, or contract, payment to a carpenter. This food gift is

known as the *fa'amoe* and is presented to a head builder (*latu*) in order to reserve his time and services as well as those of his group of workers who are
collectively known as his *au tufuga*. The request may be for the erection of a
faletele (round guest house) or a *faletofā* (long sleeping house) or a variety of
out-buildings, although these require less skill and are often built by the members
of the family themselves.

It takes between one to three months to build a Samoan house, depending on
the size and type of the dwelling, the speed of the carpenters, and whether or not
wood can be used from an old house in the construction of the new. Breadfruit,
the wood largely used in *fale* construction, is extremely durable, and the same
wood is often used in as many as three houses. Round houses are easier to build
and take less time than long houses. It is easier to find the shorter lengths of
wood used in round houses, and construction does not require the many splices
characteristic of long-house construction. All in all, the long house is a more
expensive dwelling requiring more wood, more sennit for lashings, and more labor.

The man who contracts for the building by presenting the *fa'amoe* payment to
a head carpenter is referred to as the *taufale*. When the carpenter receives the
contract gift, he distributes the food and money among his workers and sets a
day for the commencement of construction.

With this date in mind the members of the *taufale's* family begin to search for
suitable timbers. Breadfruit is preferred, but if the family lands do not contain
enough of the proper size, other woods are substituted. *Asi* (*Syzygium inophyl-
loides*) may be cut for houseposts and *Poumuli* (*Securinega* species) for house
beams. If insufficient woods are available on family lands, uncultivated bush lands
may be tapped, but these are often great distances away from the village. The
family is not only responsible for supplying a large share of the wood, but they
are responsible for providing a *tapuaiga* to insure the success of the work. A
tapuaiga (one who prays for the work) is a member of the family for whom the
house is being built who does not actually pray but merely sits and serves as a
conversationalist for the workers. He is not permitted to be critical of the quality
of the workmanship, but he probably does help to eliminate inferior performance
by his very presence. The *tapuaiga* is usually an old male, and the tales he tells
of traditional customs and the legends he relates are often of deep interest,
particularly to young carpenters.

The day that the carpenters arrive to erect the main house posts is one marked
by ceremony. This ceremony, known as the *fa'atuga o le fale* (the causing of the
house to stand upright) is attended by the carpenters, the owner's extended
family, and other chiefs who are special friends of the family. All bring food for
the owner to distribute among the carpenters and thirty fathoms of sennit apiece
to present to the owner, since the owner's family is required to provide all the
sennit used in the house lashings, and this amounts to thousands of fathoms. The
ceremony is to honor the carpenters and there are speeches by Talking Chiefs, a
presentation of kava roots to the head builder, a kava ceremony in which the
chief carpenter drinks first and receives his cup in the name of Sao, and finally a

feast in which the owner's family, the carpenters, and the village chiefs each eat in their own separate groups. When the meal is finished, the carpenters go to work. Augmenting the carpenter's crew on this first day are several other chief carpenters who volunteer their labor to get the project well under way. Collectively, this opening day work force is referred to as the "family of Sao."

After the initial ceremony, all the guests are given food gifts to take home and baskets of prized morsels are taken to the village pastor, village school teachers, the village nurse, and other important personages who were for some reason or other unable to attend.

The building of a house is a thing not taken lightly in Fitiuta. The owner (*taufale*) must constantly strive to keep the builders happy and well supplied with food and tobacco, and he usually has a member of his family prepare a bowl of kava for the workmen to drink at their leisure. Younger household members are assigned to keep a good supply of drinking nuts available to quench the workers' thirst and, of course, the owner must keep up his payments for the work.

Before the work begins there is general agreement on the price. There is also agreement on what will constitute payment. They may agree on cash, or part of the payment may be in finemats, tapa cloths, or other traditional articles of value. In addition to this, the *taufale* provides all the food for the workers while on the job. The price of a house varies according to the rank and status of the chief contracting its construction. A lower ranking chief would pay the equivalent of about $500 while a chief of high status may pay twice that amount for the same size house. If the original agreement specified that payment take place over a specific period of time, and if the owner should fail to make the proper payments on time, the carpenters might very well abandon the project. This represents a crisis situation for the owner, for under these circumstances it would be impossible to get another group of workers to finish the house. Therefore, the house would stand unfinished, a testimony to all in the village that the owner does not meet his obligations. The only way that the problem can be solved is for the owner to go to the carpenter with the promised payment plus large amounts of food, tapa cloth, finemats, and kava roots which serve as a penalty for his indiscretion.

The final day of building is again an occasion for ceremony, as well as the time when the final payment must be made to the artisans. The *taufale* once again summons his extended family to come with money and goods. The chief carpenters of the village, and often from other villages, are invited to once again make up the "family of Sao," and their only obligation is to bring kava roots and their tools for doing part of a day's work, which is more ceremonial than helpful. There is a kava ceremony in the morning, a period of work, and a good noon meal. In the afternoon chiefs from the village and from other villages arrive with goods to help their friend in his final payment and to participate in one of the more prestigious ceremonies of traditional Samoan life.

The central feature of the final day's ceremony is the payment of the *uma sa*, the final portion of the carpenter's fee. The family of the owner first presents the carpenter with a selection of mats and other household articles which are ear-marked for the carpenter's wife. Theoretically she has played an important function in the construction of the house, for in addition to her "praying" daily for the success of the work, she has helped weave units of thatch for the house, she has kept the carpenter's sleeping house clean, and she has washed the clothing of her husband's workers during the entire period of their work project. The second portion of the final payment is for the services of the head carpenter and his artisans, and it is divided among all the workers. If the payment is large, gifts will also be presented to the guest head carpenters who have gathered to celebrate the completion of the house, but if the payment is modest, the guest craftsmen will carry home only baskets of food.

4 / The world of the spirit

Christianity came to Samoa on the ship *Messenger of Peace* in the year 1830. Its apostle was an English ironmonger, John Williams, who, after establishing London Missionary Society stations in Tahiti and Rarotonga, undertook the building of a sixty-foot sailing vessel in order to expand mission operations into western Polynesia and eastern Melanesia. Sailing with Williams were Charles Barff and several Rarotongan and Tahitian missionary teachers who would pioneer the establishment of a Samoan mission. This enterprise was destined to be successful beyond expectation because of two unforeseen factors.

The first of these had to do with the party's accidental meeting with a Samoan chief by the name of Fauea when their ship called at the Wesleyan mission station in Tonga. Fauea had been converted to Christianity and now wanted passage to Samoa. Williams was happy to accommodate the new convert and was more than rewarded when they reached Samoa, for Fauea turned out to be a highly respected chief and an excellent ambassador in helping the missionaries gain rapport with the island people. A second factor which would work in William's favor became apparent upon the ship's arrival at the island of Upolu. This had to do with the recent death of the *Tamafaiga*. Williams writes that the *Tamafaiga* was a kind of prophet who had such great *mana* that he could inflict disease and even death upon those that did not comply with his wishes. Even chiefs of very high rank brought him tributes in the form of property or women. Feeling free to confiscate anything that struck his fancy, the *Tamafaiga* had very recently singled out the wife of a powerful chief as a sleeping companion. This chief, perhaps less awed by *Tamafaiga*'s *mana* than other men of rank, collected a group of fellow chiefs and together they slew the *Tamafaiga* as he lay with the woman. His body was dismembered and the skull returned to his family as evidence of the deed. This action precipitated a war of revenge which was going on when Williams arrived at Upolu.

When the Christian chief Fauea heard of the death of the *Tamafaiga*, he told Williams, "The devil is dead. Our land will now embrace the new religion." He explained that if the *Tamafaiga* were still alive he would have objected strongly to Christianity, but that now the people would accept the new religion and would never again select another *Tamafaiga*.

In 1830 the Samoan archipelago presented a different religious picture than the other areas where London Missionary Society enterprises had been started in the South Pacific. The inhabitants of the Samoan chain were referred to as the "godless Samoans" by Polynesian peoples in other parts of the Pacific. One early observer of the Samoan cultural scene maintained that while other Polynesian societies worshipped deities, the Samoans worshipped their own social and political structure.

Actually, the Samoans did have one important god, Tagaloa, and they mentioned others in their mythology, but it cannot be said that they worshipped a deity at all. The *marae* (religious centers with temples and altars) of eastern Polynesia were strangely absent in Samoa, and the priesthood, if it can be called that, consisted of chiefs (with the exception of the rather extraordinary *Tamafaiga*) who derived power more from their social and political status than from any supernatural sanction. These people were chiefs first and religious practitioners second. While there was an elaborate creation mythology, a weak concept of *mana*, and hints of totemic food observances, no one really worshipped any deity in special ceremonies. Villages or families had tutelary gods or goddesses who may have been called upon for aid in times of war or natural crisis, but there was no religious philosophy *per se* which provided moral direction or demanded ritual observance.

The focal point of village life was not a temple, but rather the *malae*, which did not serve as a holy place but rather as a village square where the village council met to decide issues of morality and to determine civil and military courses of action. It was the arena of the Chief and Talking Chief rather than that of the village priest.

To a large extent, therefore, when Williams landed his group of native missionaries from eastern Polynesia, there was little in the way of vested religious interests to deter them in their goal of spreading Christianity throughout the Navigator Islands. The Samoans had a concept of spirits, or ghosts, which they called *aitu*, but they did not see this as incompatible with a religious philosophy which stressed a spiritual life after death. Many of their minor gods became "devils" (*tiapolo*) in the new theology. The Samoans also had little in the way of "idols" or other religious paraphernalia, so they were hard pressed to demonstrate their new found faith as other Polynesian peoples had by destroying temples, altars, or pushing over *tiki* statues. Williams reports that the only direct action taken by the people upon conversion was the deliberate eating of totem animals or fish and one incident of deliberately "drowning" an old piece of matting which was purported to be the symbolic representation of a deity.

The London Mission experienced great success throughout the islands, but their religious teachings were not accepted without a great deal of deliberation and debate. Before a community decided to join the *lotu* (church), a village meeting was called by the chiefs in order to explore the issue. Williams reports lengthy deliberations revealing remarkable insight. Some chiefs urged embracing the foreign religion since it could provide them with an avenue through which to acquire valuable possessions such as belonged to the white man. Williams (1832) quotes a native chief as follows:

> Only look at the English people, they have strong beautiful clothes of various colours while we have only leaves, they have noble ships while we have only canoes, they have sharp knives while we have only bamboo to cut with, they have iron axes while we have only stones, they have scissors while we use the shark's teeth, what beautiful beads they have, looking glasses and all that is valuable. I therefore think that the God who gave them all these things must be good, and that his religion must be superior to ours. If we receive this God and worship Him, He will in time give us these things as well as them.

There is even some evidence of the development of a kind of cargo cult among these native people who seemed to be so impressed with the material wealth of Christians. Wilkes' record of his 1839 visit to Samoa carries a picture of a facsimile of a European ship being built deep in the forest. Wilkes describes the phenomenon as follows:

> An odd amusement of the natives was seen in the forest; in one of the clearings near one of the heathen villages, and at a short distance from Apia. A fine large tree had been lopt of its branches (except at the very top), for a mast; around this a framework of timber, after the model of a vessel, was constructed; all the timbers were carefully fastened together with sennit, and with the requisite curvature; from the bow a large and long piece of timber projected, and at the stern a rudder was contrived, with its tiller; but instead of its ordinary movements as with us, it was intended to act vertically, in the way to which they are accustomed in managing or steering their large canoes with an oar; vines and creepers were used for the rigging; ballast had likewise been placed in the hold.
> This afforded them great amusement, and showed an ingenuity in the construction of this Papalangi ship, as they called it, which had cost them much time and labour (1845:137).

It is tempting to interpret this unusual mock shipbuilding behavior as the kind of phenomenon which has been reported again and again in Melanesia where Christian ideas have been combined with ideas concerning the affluence and technological capabilities of the West to produce strange religious ideas about the arrival of supernatural ships and planes which will discharge vast amounts of material wealth for distribution among the faithful. Worsley (1957) and others report incidents of cargo warehouses being built to resemble airplanes or facsimilies of aircraft being constructed to serve as decoys to lure the elusive cargo carriers.

Some chiefs claimed that if all villages accepted the new religion wars would be prevented. For some, the ceremonialism of the worship services was appealing. The Samoan love and appreciation of oratory brought a favorable response from many who enjoyed listening to the almost interminable sermons delivered by the mission pastors. Even today the role of substitute pastor is one eagerly sought by village Talking Chiefs anxious to exhibit their versatility and eloquence in the area of ceremonial and formal rhetoric. Many of the chiefs took a characteristic

Samoan position in relation to the new religion—that acceptance or rejection be delayed until they knew more about it.

When Williams' ship *Messenger of Peace* called at Upolu, there were several cases of influenza among the passengers and the crew. Immediately after its departure an epidemic of the disease swept the Samoan island chain. Gray believes that the reaction to this crisis tells us something about the state of the indigenous religion. He writes:

> The Samoans' . . . acceptance of this plague, coinciding with the arrival of the *Messenger of Peace*, is evidence of the weakness of their religion, for no authoritative voice was raised to argue it was punishment for too ready acceptance of strange gods (1960:36).

Not all Samoans accepted the new religion, and in the beginning many villages were split over this issue. Whole communities held out and were described locally as being the "property of the devil." Antagonism between the saved and the unsaved often erupted into armed conflicts and had to be quelled by the missionaries working in cooperation with village chiefs.

The first formal mission station was established on the island of Ta'u in 1837 under the supervision of a Rarotongan and a Tahitian mission teacher. By 1840 the London Missionary Society characterized the Manu'a Group as one of its principal strongholds.

In order to understand many of the attitudes and activities of the modern church in Samoa it is necessary to know something of the values held by the early missionaries who first brought Christianity to the area. All of the early English missionaries seemed to be unable to separate their religious beliefs from their cultural values. John Williams, for example, believed that sloth was the deadliest of sins and saw it as a paramount responsibility to keep the people busy, partly to keep idle hands from devil's purposes and partly to insure sizable donations to the church. In 1825 the native London Missionary Society congregation at Raiatea, in the Society islands, was commanded by missionaries to build a larger church, although the one they had built five years earlier was more than adequate for their needs. Such demands were communicated to Samoans as well, and a church-building mania—still evident today—began.

Education was always tied to proselytizing. During the middle and late 1830s missionaries devised a written form of the Samoan language, printed religious tracts—usually portions of the Bible—and began forming classes to teach the people to read and study the truths of the Christian theology. Charles Wilkes estimated in 1839 that there were approximately 10,000 literate Samoans. The reason for this was that the ability to read was a prerequisite for church membership.

The Samoans were quick to appreciate the new mythology taught by the mission teachers, the sermons, and the ceremonialism of the liturgy. The Bible stories were added to the oral literature and Talking Chiefs found new avenues for achievement—delivering sermons on Sunday mornings or serving as elders or deacons in the village church organization. In a culture where speechmaking had traditionally accompanied any formal gathering, long sermons involving even a new set of gods and heroes found compatibility with existing cultural forms. In addition to the ritual of the kava ceremony, the people now had Communion, and they immediately took to the new symbols and trappings which adorned the church interiors. Generosity in gift exchange had always been an admired quality, and Christianity provided the opportunity of acquiring additional respect from one's fellows by lavish giving to the church.

The prophets of the new god—sometimes Europeans and sometimes native mission teachers from Tahiti or Rarotonga—quickly impressed upon their converts the "Thou shall nots" of the new religion. This was not novel either, for although *tapu* was not as strong a concept in Samoa as in eastern Polynesia, it was however recognized. Christian *tapu* priorities seemed to rest in the area of sex and family relations, and Samoans were directed to abolish such practices as polygamy, divorce, political marriages, marriages between Christians and non-Christians, adultery, premarital sex relations, lavish gift exchanges at marriages, the public test of virginity, and prostitution. Violation of any of the tenets of the church meant expulsion from membership. Somewhat less serious, but of great enough import to warrant special attention from missionaries, was the matter of nudity. New standards designated "full coverage" for women, and for men, who normally covered what the missionaries considered the necessary areas in their everyday dress, special church dress of shirts, ties, and often coats was prescribed in addition to ankle-length wrap-arounds (*lavalava*) of cotton trade cloth.

Beyond the sphere of family life there was yet a greater list of *tapu* behavior. War and violence were forbidden except in defense of life or property. Consumption of liquor and kava and the use of tobacco was prohibited. There was to be no gambling, tattooing, bush medicine, or sorcery, and funeral feasts, which missionaries considered wasteful, were discouraged as much as possible.

In exchange for all these prohibitions the Samoans received literacy; the idea of the dignity of work; new ceremonialism in the form of christenings, weddings, funerals, and Communion; new songs to sing with strange new harmony; and the promise of salvation in a hereafter which resembled, in some ways, the Pulotu that they had believed in for centuries. What Samoans probably expected, although the European missionaries were not aware of it, was that ultimately they would also acquire some of the white man's magic for getting material wealth.

In 1845 a seminary known as Malua College was established on the island of Upolu, and the London Missionary Society began training its own Samoan teachers and village pastors (*faifeau*). The graduates of this school were supposed to be paid a salary of ten pounds a year, but good intentions soon outstripped the London Missionary Society coffers, and individual villages were made responsible for the support of the local pastor. This system still prevails. Village pastors receive their salary from church donations, and in many villages the pastor and his family are provided with all of their food, each family taking a turn supplying and even cooking daily sustenance.

In order to understand the nature of the Samoan religious system today, it is important to know something of the indigenous beliefs, as there are numerous survivals of those beliefs in contemporary Samoan religion. Traditional understandings have also led to reinterpretations of Christian doctrines.

As has been pointed out earlier, John Williams found Samoa without idols, altars, or priests and without formal worship of the gods. Williams' journal alludes only to "mouth worship," that is, prayers uttered in low muttering terms in times of crisis, such as the serious illness of a relative. Other observers tell of prayers to village or household gods being said prior to family meals. Since this practice was apparently traditional, we are somewhat less impressed by missionary claims of "great success" in teaching Samoans to offer prayers of thanksgiving for their daily bread.

While the names of a large number of Polynesian gods are included in Samoan myths, their supreme god and creator was Tagaloa. Elsewhere in Polynesia this deity had a restricted sphere of influence, being primarily the god of the sea and fishermen. The Samoans believed in a Tagaloa family who lived on ten mountains which they referred to as *lagi* (heavens). The most important of the Tagaloas was Tagaloa Lefuli (unchangeable) who was also known by the names Tagaloa Mana (powerful) and Tagaloa Fa'atutupunu'u (creator). Within the Tagaloa pantheon were such deities as Tagaloa Pule (authority), Tagaloa Tetea (albino), Tagaloa Tula'i (standing) and Tagaloa Savalivali, the messenger of the gods.

Tagaloas were not worshipped, although the early literature implied that prayers were often offered up, or feast foods were dedicated to them. References to the ancient gods are made during various phases of the kava ceremony even today. Tagaloa had no priests and whatever attention was paid to the deity was from family heads or orator chiefs whose religious office was a part of their normal role as titled elite.

Tagaloa gods, collectively known as *atua*, were the highest of two classes of supernatural beings. Below the Tagaloa deities was a class of national, village, and family spirits referred to as *aitu*. Most *aitu* were believed to be the spirits of dead ancestors and had only local significance for particular families or villages, but there was a large class of *aitu* which had national significance. Examples of the latter were Tuiatua, Sauma'eafe, Saveasiuleo, Nafanua, and Nifoloa. Some of these spirits are averred even today, and older villagers often are able to identify sacred places or objects which the spirits occupy.

Tuiatua is believed to have a special association with Fitiuta, although he may travel about the entire Samoan archipelago. This is the spirit of a human being who once lived in Fitiuta on a section of land known as Mutie. One old chief maintained that he always knew when the spirit was about by the sound of his staff on the village path. Returning bonito boats dedicate their catch to this spiritual being.

Sauma'eafe also was once a mortal who lived in the Manu'a island group. It is said that while still a girl she was stolen by *aitu* and changed into a spirit. Like other *aitu* she has the power to possess and speak through people.

Saveasi'uleo is a spirit who presides over Pulotu, the realm of Samoan afterlife. His daughter, Nafanua, a kind of Samoan Joan of Arc, left Pulotu in mythical times to lead the people against an oppressive political regime. In a great battle in which her forces were victorious she wrapped coconut leaves about her body so the enemy would not discover her sex. After the battle she made the vanquished wrap the trunks of coconut trees with palm fronds, thereby symbolically designating her ownership of the land and its products. The practice is still followed today in the form of a charm (*tapui*) used by land owners to protect their coconuts from theft.

Nifoloa, the long toothed demon, was a disease- and death-dealing spirit. One disease, which carries the name of this *aitu*, is still much feared throughout Samoa. It is believed that once one has contracted Nifoloa, the slightest scratch will produce a serious infection which in most cases leads to death. In one of the villages in Manu'a the grave of a Nifoloa victim is carefully bordered with red flowers so that people will avoid it, for even coming near the grave of one of its victims is supposedly sufficient contact to contract the disease.

All the above spirits are classed under the term *folauga aitu* and are believed to be capable of travelling throughout the Samoan chain. They are purported to be able to take the form of birds, fish, reptiles, human beings, or to remain invisible if they choose. They possess men and women and often speak through them and affect their behavior—a phenomenon which becomes a convenient rationalization for departures from prescribed Christian behavior.

There were also lesser *aitu* associated with only one village or one family. These often appeared to people in the form of birds, animals, or fish and were undoubtedly the basis for food *tapus* which have been interpreted as totemic observances. Little remains of these ideas today, but there are villages and families in Samoa who have traditionally refrained from eating particular land or sea creatures although they are not certain exactly why they are thus restricted.

The kind of *aitu* which are universally accepted in modern Samoa are the ghosts of ancestors, sometimes benevolent, sometimes mischievous, and sometimes malevolent. They are believed capable of appearing in recognizable human form, but at night they invariably wear white. There are places traditionally recognized as gathering spots for such ghosts, and few people care to dally while passing such haunts. Almost without exception Samoans can relate eerie and often terrifying experiences they have had with these spirit beings. *Aitu* tales are so commonplace that even Europeans become affected. The following is from an official Public Health Department report written in 1950. It describes the *aitu* troubles encountered by the United States Navy pharmacist's mates stationed on the island of Ofu, some seven miles distant from the village of Fitiuta.

The dispensary in the Island of Ofu is the only building belonging to the Public Health Department which has been the recipient of ghostly visitations. The site of the building erected in 1923 was Toaga, Ofu, selected because it was convenient for Ofu islanders and also for those of the neighboring island of

Olosega. The two are separated by only about 100 yards of water, and it is possible to wade across at low tide.

At once the people of both islands protested, saying Toaga was well known to be the meeting place of the *aitu* (evil spirits) of the whole of the Manu'a Group. After the dispensary was built they refused to visit it.

One night, about 1924 (according to the story) the pharmacist's mate on duty was called to the door by someone knocking. When he opened up, nobody was to be seen. The knocking was repeated nightly for a while. One night on opening the door, he beheld the apparition of a headless man. Next day, when he was gone on a call, his wife was harrassed by unseen persons who, in broad daylight, tramped noisily through the house and moved the furniture about.

Soon after, the pharmacist's mate and his wife, with the two nurses, went to Ofu. They were offered a return ride that night in the longboat of a High Chief. The party set out on the four mile journey to Toaga, leaving the nurses, who were to follow on foot next day. When the boat approached the haunted spot, a horrid sight met their eyes. On the moonlit beach a *siva* was in progress, and obscene, headless figures danced, led by the nurses they had just left at Ofu.

While the veracity of this story has been denied, the fact remains that before long the dispensary was torn down and moved to Ofu village. The Medical Practitioner whose duties take him past Toaga says that even today, the old women caution him not to pass by at high noon or at night.

Even the new dispensary at Ofu village is not free from contact with the other world, but now in an amiable form. Foisia, an elderly spirit with a long white beard, who inhabits a rocky islet just off the coast of Ofu, is said to pay the dispensary an occasional visit. Apparently the pharmacist's mates on duty there in recent years have not recognized him (1950:4).

According to common belief most *aitu* cause trouble only if their families are engaging in activities of which they do not approve or if they died in a distant village or country. The latter belief has led to some reticence on the part of the seriously ill to go to the hospital on Tutuila for treatment.

When *aitu* bring misfortune to families with whom they are displeased it is usually in the form of an illness known as *ma'i aitu* (spirit sickness) and involves the symptoms of delirium, chills, sleep walking, and sudden, aimless running about. Village specialists in *aitu* medicine, known as *taulāsea*, treat these spirit maladies with various leaf and herb concoctions. Recoveries may also come about as a result of a family changing its ways or reversing a decision which they believe might have precipitated the wrath of the spirit.

Numerous precautions are taken to protect against the possibility of contact with *aitu*. For example, a single house blind (*pola*) left up when all the rest are lowered is an invitation for a spirit to enter the *fale*. If two blinds on opposite sides of the house are left up *aitu* will invariably walk through the house, and sleepers lying in their path will wake up feeling sore and tired as if someone had walked over them throughout the night.

Even before the coming of the Christian missionary, Samoans believed in an immortal soul (*agaga*) which left the body at the time of death and journeyed either to Pulotu or to Fafā. Pulotu was known as the "abode of the blessed." It was described to Charles Wilkes in 1839 as "an island to the westward," where "the spirit goes immediately after death"; a place where "it never rains," where people "eat and drink without labor," and where they are "waited upon by beautiful women, who are always young" and "whose breasts never hang down" (1845:132). While Wilkes was told that Pulotu was an island to the westward, the more common belief was that it lay beneath the sea just beyond the end of Savai'i and was entered by way of two whirlpools—one for chiefs and one for the untitled.

Fafā was the Samoan Hades, a place of dread and punishment ruled over by O le Fe'e (octopus). Early literature tells us little concerning who was assigned to this afterworld or why, and its location has been described merely as "westward of Savai'i." It is likely that after the coming of the missionaries Fafā was quickly conceptualized as being identical with Satan's domain. Although souls were permanently committed to these afterworlds, they were apparently free to return on occasion to their earthly village homes where they would appear in ghostly form to family members or intervene in the lives of surviving kinsmen.

Mana and *tapu* seem strangely unimportant in Samoa when compared with eastern Polynesia. Samoans have always thought in terms of sacred *fono* (village councils) rather than sacred chiefs. Agricultural lands or fishing areas on the reef flat were (and still are) made *tapu* if there was danger of depleting resources when a large feast or celebration was anticipated, but these restrictions were imposed by the village council and not by an individual chief or by a deity. There were vague suggestions that paramount chiefs had more *mana* than regular chiefs and that chiefs of any degree had more than untitled persons, but *mana* was only an important consideration where royal titles such as the Tuimanu'a or the Malietoa were concerned. The Tuimanu'a, for example, had to be served meals by his wife who had comparable *mana* or by serving people who had been ceremonially rendered immune to the force of his inherent power. Since no such title as the Tuimanu'a exists today, and since most ideas of *mana* were associated with titles rather than persons, these concepts have now disappeared. In Western Samoa special precautions against the force of *mana* inherent in royal titles like Malietoa and Mata'afa have also become a thing of the past.

In regard to the concept of *tapu* and *mana*, Margaret Mead points out that

> with the absence of any sort of primogeniture, no special sanctity of the first born, and the late accession to a title, men who would later hold high rank, lived and mingled with common men for the first twenty-five to thirty-five years of their lives.
>
> Except for the tapus of the Tui Manua and the few tapus of other High Chiefs, those observances: respect for the garments, food, bed, cup name of the chiefs, which were motivated in other parts of Polynesia by the fear of the contagious sanctity of the chief, became mere etiquette. Even the sanctity of the Tui Manua was invaded by this iconoclastic conception. A man who was to be Tui Manua might be tattooed before he acceded to the title but not afterward. Children born to him before accession were treated as other children; children born to him afterward were *tama paia* (sacred children). Intrinsic sanctity of persons— not of the mere present incumbants of titles—was foreign to the Samoan feeling (1930:122).

Among the survivals of indigenous belief is the concept of *tapui*. This idea, originally noted by George Turner during his period of mission service in Samoa (1842–1859), involves what Turner (1884) calls a class of "curses" used as a protection for property. He lists eight such "curses" which might better have been labelled "protective charms." They are the sea-pike, the white shark, the cross-stick, the ulcer, the tic-doloureux, the death, the rat, and the thunder *tapui*. Over a hundred years later at least two of these—the sea-pike and the rat *tapui*—are still being used to protect property.

In the case of the rat *tapui*, a small coconut leaf basket filled with *vaofali* or *vaolima* weeds is hung on a coconut tree to protect plantation land from damage and theft. Violation results in damage being done by rats to the clothing, tapa, or finemats of the guilty party. The sea-pike, or swordfish, *tapui* consists of half a coconut frond braided into a facsimile of a swordfish which, like the basket, is hung on a tree to protect agricultural land. The charm threatens the thief with impalement by the swordfish on his next entrance into the sea. The same general concept is retained in several new *tapui* which have been developed in modern times. Among these are the boil *tapui*, the hernia *tapui*, the general sickness *tapui* and the *tuia* (skin disease) *tapui*. Each of these charms threatens various forms of physical ailments if ownership rights to land or other forms of personal or family property are violated.

THE CONTEMPORARY SAMOAN CHURCH

Samoans, like many people of the non-Western world, seem capable of compartmentalizing Christian and indigenous beliefs so that what appear to be contradictions in the two systems do not seem to cause any anxiety or conflict. Although nearly all modern Samoans identify as Christians, there is still widespread knowledge of indigenous mythology and spirit lore. While all Christians subscribe to the scriptural belief in a Heaven and a Hell, there are few Samoans who would not recognize the word *Pulotu* or have some knowledge of traditional beliefs concerning its characteristics. When the author asked an elderly Talking Chief (who had just spent several hours describing the Tagaloa pantheon) if he believed in the veracity of the Book of Genesis, he stated that he believed every word of it. When he was asked how he reconciled this belief with the story of how Tagaloa had created the Samoan islands and its inhabitants, the Talking Chief replied that the story of creation as it appeared in the Bible explained the origin of the white man, but that he was absolutely convinced that Tagaloa was the creator of the Samoan people and the islands they inhabited.

While the majority of Samoans are enthusiastic supporters of the modern church, European observers have expressed some doubt as to the depth and quality of Samoan Christianity. An example is found in the statement of a missionary quoted by Felix Keesing:

> I am afraid that from the Christian viewpoint the missions have been rather a failure in Samoa. Instead of accepting Christianity and allowing it to remold

their lives to its form, the Samoans have fitted them inside Samoan custom, making them a part of the native culture (1934:410).

Of course, the phenomenon of a particular culture "swallowing up" or reinterpreting a foreign theology so that it meets the needs of the society is not unique to the Samoan situation. Indeed, it probably has happened wherever Christianity (a Middle Eastern religion) has spread throughout the world.

Over the years any number of denominational groups have tried their hand at molding religious belief and worship in Samoa. The Wesleyan Mission, which is known as *lotu toga* (The Tongan Church), was established by Peter Turner in 1835, approximately a year earlier than the arrival of the first resident European missionaries of the London Missionary Society. Wesleyan native teachers began working in the Manu'a Group as early as 1828, but their effect was minimal. More effective was the London Missionary Society convert named Hura who was shipwrecked on Ta'u Island sometime during the 1820s. With great zeal and a portion of the Tahitian Bible he managed to salvage, he immediately set about instructing the people of Ta'u in the new religion.

Roman Catholic Marist missionaries arrived in Samoa in 1845, but most of their influence has been confined to Savai'i, Upolu, and Tutuila. The Manu'a Group has remained fiercely loyal to the London Missionary Society from the very beginning. They have tolerated the few Roman Catholic families who live among them and have permitted occasional visits to their villages by priests, but there are no Roman Catholic houses of worship in Manu'a nor any other evidence that the Roman church has had much success in terms of converts.

Mormon missionaries began working on Tutuila in 1888 and on Ta'u Island in 1904 but found a mission field that was far from fertile. Elder Workman, the first Latter Day Saints missionary in Manu'a, after a period of three months, complained of strong opposition by the chiefs and even the Tuimanu'a. Meetings, he claimed, were broken up and those in attendance were fined or otherwise punished. Mormon missionaries have been stationed in Fitiuta for several years, but their work has generally met with little success. Other denominations such as Nazarene, Seventh Day Adventist, Four Square Gospel, and several varieties of Pentecostal churches have sent missionaries to American Samoa, but none of these have carried on any proselytizing in the Manu'a Group. Margaret Mead found a Bahai unit in Ta'u village, however, when she revisited the locale of her *Coming of Age in Samoa* study in 1971.

Church membership in American Samoa remains dominantly London Missionary Society with approximately seventy-seven percent of the population. Roman Catholics make up thirteen percent, Mormons six percent, Wesleyans three percent, and all others one percent. These figures are for American Samoa as a whole. While accurate statistics do not exist for the Manu'a situation, it might be estimated that this area contains a higher percentage of London Missionary Society members than the average.

The church started by native teachers of the London Missionary Society in

1830 is known today as The Congregational Christian Church of Samoa. It has seven districts in Western Samoa and one in American Samoa. The church is self-governing and self-supporting. Although it is a member of the International Congregational Council and the World Council of Churches, there are no European or American church representatives in residence in Samoa. The church today sends its own missionaries to Niue, the Gilbert, Ellice, and Tokelau islands and to New Guinea.

Although there is a church organization which encompasses the entire Samoan archipelago, each individual village church enjoys a great deal of autonomy. Native pastors (*faifeau*) serve and are supported by the community. While these men cannot be titled, they hold a status equal to or greater than chiefs, and they are normally in attendance whenever the village council convenes. Their views carry great weight and their advice and leadership is highly valued.

The Fitiuta church organization consists of a group of elders, deacons, and the *Ekalesia* (ecclesiastical membership). Elders and deacons are invariably titled individuals and such offices are important to personal and family prestige. As in many Protestant church organizations, elders are the decision-makers and supervisors of spiritual affairs, and the deacons are the keepers of the church treasury and administrators of church property.

The members of the *Ekalesia* make up the preferred membership role of the church. These are the people who have undergone a period of instruction called the *Sāiliili* and consequently adhere to a specific set of beliefs and code of behavior. In addition to the requirement of attending church regularly, they are forbidden to drink alcoholic beverages, attend movies, or participate in European-style social dancing. Their lives must be beyond reproach morally, and they are expected to give sizable donations to the church on a regular basis. Members of the *Ekalesia* (which include the elders and deacons) are the only ones permitted to partake in Communion when it is served on the first Sunday of every month. Any violation of the behavioral code of the *Ekalesia* results in the offender being removed from membership. Reinstatement comes only after an additional period of instruction and the permission of the entire membership.

Samoan churches are European in architectural design with cement or limestone walls, corrugated iron roofs, and elaborate folk-art interiors involving wood inlay designs and windows with stained glass panes. Altars are often draped with appliquéd or embroidered hangings and decorated with artificial flower arrangements and religious pictures of conservative European style. Most churches have pews, a Communion table (used mostly for collection of the church offering), a pulpit, and an altar. Ventilation is poor and most sanctuaries are uncomfortable, as the architecture is ill-suited to the tropical climate (one of the more vital items of church-going equipment is a coconut leaf fan). Early missionary accounts speak of construction of early churches which replicated the Samoan *fale*, but evidently as the new religion grew in favor, the prestige of European style churches also increased and soon the English country church design, often with a touch of Spanish influence, became standard in every Samoan village.

SUNDAY IN SAMOA

Sunday begins early in Fitiuta—about 5 A.M.—with the ringing of the church bell. Even at this early hour there is already activity in the village. Columns of smoke ascend from the cook houses of most household clusters of buildings. Since Sabbath cooking must be completed before daybreak, a significant number of young men and women have already been preparing the day's food for at least an hour. For others, the bells represent ample announcement of the first service of the day which takes place at six o'clock. There will be sufficient time to open the large wooden trunks which hold Sunday clothing, select the proper attire, press out the wrinkles with a charcoal-heated iron, consume a piece of cold cooked taro or a cooked green banana, and still be punctual for the early church service. Attendance at this service is light—the majority of worshippers preferring the eight o'clock hour. In the thirty to forty minute interval between services the village choir congregates in the *fale* of one of its members and runs through a last minute rehearsal of the morning choral selections. Their main rehearsal takes place earlier in the week. In most of the *fales* in the village the church-goers wait until the last minute before putting on their Sunday best so that it will not become wrinkled in the humid heat of the morning. Young women carefully dress their hair in braids and pin on their low-crowned, wide-brimmed coconut hats. Everyone carries a coconut frond basket just the right size to hold a Bible and a hymnal. The chiefs wear white *lavalavas*, shirts, and cotton coats and solid black ties. Untitled men often leave the coat at home and occasionally sport a flowered or striped tie. Unmarried women wear a knee-length cotton frock (usually white), but married women find it proper to wear a *pulatasi*, that is, a two-tiered costume consisting of an ankle-length *lavalava* overlaid with a thigh-length cotton dress, all in white.

At approximately 7:45 A.M. the church bell rings again and the church procession begins. Whole families emerge from their household dwellings and walk leisurely and single file along the narrow concrete pathway that cuts through the heart of the village of Fitiuta. As the families enter the church the members disperse, the women filling in the right side of the sanctuary, the men the left, and the children taking seats in the middle. On the left and right sides at the front are special pews for the more important chiefs and their wives, and directly in front of the pulpit is a section reserved for the choir. This is also the location of a small pump organ which is often played by the choir director who seems to be able ingeniously to conduct and play simultaneously.

At the back of the children's section two elderly men station themselves. Equipped with canes, they are there to maintain order among the youngsters who are prone to forget proper church decorum. Whispers or nodding heads are often responded to with a gentle but unmistakable rap on the top of the cranium dispensed by one of the elderly monitors.

The service begins with a hymn and a prayer followed by a responsive reading from the Samoan Bible. A hymn which follows this reading is more in the form of an anthem, and this is the choir's opportunity to perform. The words are often direct translations of traditional Protestant hymns, but the melodies are frequently different. Harmonically, Samoan church music differs little from Western religious music, but the tonal quality and musical style are uniquely Polynesian. The women sing in high nasal voices, while the men carry the lower parts with full, deep tones. The female voices carry the melody and the male voices provide a moving bass line which complements and yet provides a contrapuntal contrast with the lead voices. Few Samoans read music, and hymnals do not include musical notation. Most melodies are traditional and familiar to everyone. The ability to sing in three part harmony seems to come easily to Samoans, although the indigenous music of this area did not feature harmony. Traditional chants of various kinds were characterized by a narrow range in melody, carefully enunciated texts, and well coordinated unison rendition.

Samoan church music, highly influenced by European modes in its structure, differs greatly in performance in that it tends to be joyful, rhythmic, and loud. More likely than not it resembles the vocal music used to accompany the Samoan dance, the *siva*.

The morning sermon is probably the highlight of the service. Rich in parables and Old Testament biblical history, the sermon stresses proper behavior, piety, and the wages of sin. In a society which has developed oratory as its highest art, the minister is valued for his rhetorical skill and style and for the content of his message. Sermons are normally lengthy and are concluded with a prayer. When the final hymn of the morning draws to a close and the worshippers close their hymnals, the deacons station themselves at a long table in front of the Communion rail and begin the reading of the church roll. When each family name is called, a representative of that family comes forward and lays its morning offering on the table. The amount is observed by a deacon, recorded in a book, and announced to the congregation. In a status-oriented society like Samoa, where generosity is praised, Sunday morning offerings are substantial.

After the service, families return home and quickly change into less elegant attire and prepare to eat their morning meal which was cooked well before daybreak. The *matai* of each family does not share this meal, for he and the other *matai* of the village gather in the *fale* of one of their number, eat together, and discuss things trivial and profound well into the afternoon.

Sundays are for rest and relaxation. The women of the village take long strolls with neighbors, children go down to the beach and play in the surf, and elders take long naps or sit quietly carrying on lengthy conversations with friends or family members. No work is done, and the village remains quiet and lethargic.

The church bell tolls again at 4 o'clock announcing the afternoon service. In form it is much like the one held in the morning, but it tends to attract fewer worshippers and those who appear are more informally dressed. Men arrive in shirt sleeves and women wear simple flowered dresses. There is usually a noticeable absence of teenage children at this service, for they have one of their own two hours later.

The evening is again the time for strolling and conversation, for a cool bath at the village bathing pool and an early retirement. For most, the new work week will begin before dawn with a journey to the plantations high on the slope and a morning of cultivation before the advent of the noonday heat.

THE CHURCH DEDICATION

Samoans have often been accused of having a church-building obsession. An object of village pride in every community, the church is a symbol of religious commitment. It is often claimed that the completion of one church is the signal to start planning for a new and bigger one. Originally encouraged by John Williams to insure proper industry among new converts, church building has become a major prestige activity. Without doubt, a church dedication is the most gala event that occurs in modern Samoa, with the possible exception of the annual government-sponsored Flag Day celebrations in American Samoa.

For Fitiuta the church dedication at Fagasā village on Tutuila had special meaning. The Fagasā pastor was a member of a Fitiuta family and therefore Fitiuta was expected to play a major role in the celebration. The Fagasā church was twenty-five years old and had been declared inadequate for its growing congregation. Construction had been underway on a new, much larger church for nearly a year. The date for the dedication of the new facility had been set well in advance, for elaborate plans had to be made to insure a proper celebration. In every village in Samoa congregations were collecting money so that a dedication donation might be made in the name of their village.

A week prior to the event the interisland vessel began making daily trips to Western Samoa to transport the guests, and two trips were made to Manu'a. The village of Fitiuta was sending a delegation of one hundred people, most of which was made up of a choir which would perform a specially composed anthem of commemoration. The group brought live pigs, hundreds of pounds of keg beef, and other foods, and their spokesman, a High Talking Chief, carried an envelope which contained Fitiuta's dedication contribution of $1000. The transportation costs of the group amounted to an additional $800.

Three other villages also sent large choirs, each with its own original dedication song. All in all, over 2000 guests were in attendance when the first of the two-day dedication event dawned. The morning hours were occupied with a great kava ceremony. While chiefs of the many villages partook of the ceremonial drink and listened to speeches of welcome and speeches of eulogy for guests and church builders alike, the chief's wives sought the shade of Fagasā's *fales* where they sat for hours chatting with friends and relatives whom they had not seen for

Processional to the village church for dedication ceremony.

some time. People continued to arrive throughout the entire day, and the song contest, originally planned to begin at 2 P.M. did not get underway until nearly 4:30.

The four competing choirs, numbering nearly one hundred singers each, seated themselves on the grass of the village *malae*. Each had its own set of uniforms made specially for the occasion. Women wore print dresses and men were attired in matching *lavalavas* and cotton shirts.

Songs were lengthy and narrative in form. They told the story of the history of the building project—who had helped raise the money, who the carpenters were, and how the new church would enhance the work of God's kingdom. After each song the group's contribution to the expense of the new church was presented and each donation was accompanied by a lengthy formal oration.

After all the choirs had performed their special songs, the mood of the celebration changed. The choral groups now sang songs to accompany dance performances of their village *taupou* and *manaia*. Since it is generally accepted that church dedications are supposed to be joyous occasions, the guests encouraged the dancers and singers to perform another and then another lively selection. Finally a prominent Fagasā church official came forward and the dancing stopped. He announced that Fitiuta had won the song contest. It was an honor they would long cherish and allude to in future dedication anthems.

In the evening of the first day the women of the host village presented a *konsieti,* a classic play with music featuring elaborate costumes, a large cast, and a plot out of Roman mythology. After the play there was group dancing and singing, and it was nearly dawn before all the Coleman lanterns were turned down and the village guests were settled for the night on the sleeping mats provided by their hosts.

The actual ceremony of church dedication officially took place at 11 A.M. of the second day when, after a long series of congratulatory speeches by *faifeau* from various villages, the Chief Justice of the Government of American Samoa led a procession to the new church and unlocked the doors. Returning to the *malae,* the church officials read the long list of contributors of money gifts, village by village, person by person. When the roll had been read, Fitiuta had won still another honor. They had made the largest total donation of any village.

The gala two-day celebration ended with a performance of the combined choirs of all the villages in attendance, their volume literally vibrating the structure of the newly built church. And then it was over and families began to leave the village on foot, by bus, and automobile on the road that led over the mountain to Pago Pago. A $28,000 church had been dedicated in a magnificent ceremony which had brought donations of $18,000 plus a lot of love and good will. The Fagasā church was the newest and grandest on the island of Tutuila, but probably not for long.

5 / The day to day world—life cycle

Children are born today in the village dispensary with the assistance of a Samoan graduate nurse. The village of Ta'u, some five miles away, has a small hospital with a Samoan medical practitioner in residence, so many mothers choose to be driven over the mountainous road in the government vehicle and stay with relatives for several days until their labor begins. Most expectant mothers prefer the security and familiarity of their own village, however, and settle for the services of the well-trained and experienced nurse. Not so many years ago all births took place in the household *fale* with a midwife in attendance. Mead describes the traditional procedure as follows,

> The birth takes place upon a piece of bark cloth specially prepared for the occasion. Three positions of delivery are recognized: kneeling, lying on the back, and sitting squatting on one of the logs (about two feet long and seven inches in diameter) which stand between the house posts. The last is the preferred position. The birth of the first child is always regarded as the most difficult and the birth of a girl believed to produce harder labor than the birth of a boy (1930:37).

After the mother had delivered, the midwife cut the umbilical cord and cleansed the head of the child by sucking out its eyes and nose and licking its face. A child who responded to this treatment with lusty wails was pronounced strong and healthy. The newborn was then totally bathed in warm water, wrapped in white barkcloth, and laid on its own pile of tiny sleeping mats. Then the mother was massaged and bathed.

When the well-being of the mother and child were assured, thoughts turned to determining the child's future by proper disposition of the umbilical cord.

Here modern thinking differs little from that of midwife days. To bury a piece of the cord near the oven guarantees that a boy will mature into a good cook and an industrious plantation worker. More often the cord is buried near the church in the belief that such action will result in the child (of either sex) growing into a pious and intelligent adult. Mainly there is concern that the cord be safeguarded lest a rat get it and thereby result in the child's growing up to be dull-witted and troublesome. These ideas would seem to be related to earlier traditional notions concerning the severing of the cord. Earlier generations believed that an umbilical cord cut on a war club would ultimately produce a brave warrior, while one cut on a *siapo* board would insure that a girl would grow into an adult with ability and industry in women's activities.

Children are named by the parents soon after birth, often receiving familiar names like *Lupe* (pigeon), *Pepe* (butterfly), *Matagi* (wind), *Galu* (wave), or such compound names as *Fasialofa* (go with love), *Sililavalesauilefamema'i* (its better to come to the hospital) or *Asoluafuluvaluome* (28th day of May). Biblical names are popular, the most common being *Ioane* (John), *Paulo* (Paul), and *Iosefa* (Joseph). Sharing this popularity are names derived from events occurring at the time of the birth. The name *Sanoma*, for example, was given one male child because a ship of that named arrived in Pago Pago on his birthday. European influence is becoming apparent in the naming process, as more and more parents select such names as *Telefone* (telephone), *Kerosine* (Kerosene), and *Kalinekesi* (Kleenex). Children are often named for dead ancestors in order to keep their memory alive, but the practice of naming a son after his father is not followed. Once selected, names are recorded with the village pastor, the "mayor" (*pulenu'u*), and with the medical personnel at the dispensary.

The birth of a child is an occasion for a feast, particularly if the child is born into a family of high rank. First births are always celebrated, but there is an increasing tendency to celebrate all births. These feasts are accompanied by an exchange of property between the families of the child's father and mother, the former's family bringing a category of gifts known as *oloa* (see p. 50) and the latter's reciprocating with *toga*. *Toga* goods consist of baby sleeping mats, bits of cloth in which to wrap the baby, and, in families of high rank, even finemats. Food and money are the offerings of the father's people. The kinsmen bring their gifts, give them, and return with gifts of equal value, but the parents of the child profit not at all and the child only slightly. The important thing is that an occasion of note has been celebrated with an exchange of property, formal speeches, and a generous sharing of food.

For the first four or five months the child is fed only mother's milk, and it is nursed whenever it cries. It is constantly attended to, rocked to sleep at night, and showered with love and affection. About the fourth month solid food in the form of mashed papaya, taro, banana, or soft bits of fish is introduced, but children are not completely weaned until they are approximately a year old. Even then weaning is not traumatic and in some cases nursing may extend as long as twenty-two months. The weaning experience usually involves separating the child from the mother for three or four days. During this time the child is placed in the care of its father or removed altogether from the household and placed with a grandmother or other relative. When the child desires liquid it is given a cup of water, and when it returns to its mother, if there is still a yearning for the breast, it is sometimes given but with the nipple smeared with lime juice.

A mother with a newborn is not expected to engage in agricultural activities for a period of four to six months, but then she resumes work with the rest of the family on their plantation land and the child is left with a sibling or an elderly member of the household. This results in irregular feeding since the mother is often unable to nurse the child for intervals of from six to eight hours. The problem of irregular and inadequate feeding becomes even more acute after weaning, since it is a common pattern to turn the care of infants totally over to older siblings often only five or six years the baby's senior. If the older child is not attentive to how much nourishment the baby is getting, serious health problems can result. Malnutrition combined with other complications (usually of a respiratory nature) take a heavy toll of children during the beginning months of their second year of life.

There is a great tendency to overdress small children in dresses, bonnets, blankets, and even long stockings, and this promotes excessive perspiration and encourages rashes and other skin diseases. As children grow older, they are dressed in less and less, and it is not unusual for healthy robust youngsters to go completely naked from about four months to two years of age. A tiny shirt may be their only concession to modesty.

Small children are bathed daily. The child is usually held in a standing position while the mother dumps a coffee can full of water over its head and liberally lathers the child from head to toe. Finally a cascade of fresh cold water from the can removes the soap from the inevitably screaming child. Mothers have a unique method of removing soap and water from the baby's eyes. They place their lips against the eye socket and blow, thereby forcing water and suds out of the corner of the eye. Following the bath, the child is dried with a towel and rubbed with coconut oil.

Toilet training begins at about one year of age. Prior to this time the mother merely wipes up the mat after each elimination, for Samoan babies wear no diapers. When the mother decides that training should start, she merely sets the child outside the house whenever it begins to urinate or defecate. Children who fail to learn from this gentle persuasion are often spanked, since parents believe that their failures result from laziness rather than lack of knowledge or training. Since most adults eliminate in the bush themselves, toilet training is mostly a matter of teaching the child to respect the inside of the house.

Most children learn to walk at about one year of age, but slow walkers are given special treatment. Mothers take them to the beach where they bury them hip deep in the sand. They are allowed to stand for several minutes with the support of the sand and then are violently jerked out. This is believed to make a child walk within a week or two, but if this fails the mother takes the child out on the reef flat and swings it back and forth several times allowing its buttocks and legs to strike the surface of the water.

Samoan tots begin to talk at about eighteen months of age. Many parents encourage them by saying words for the youngsters to repeat, these words often being *ai* (eat), *inu* (drink), or *moe* (sleep). Such words are taught early with the idea that it will be an aid in understanding the child's physical needs. Personal names of parents and siblings are learned early, but kinship terms in general are not mastered until late childhood.

A child no sooner learns to walk than he is also taught that it is bad manners to walk or stand up inside the house, because a child's head is never supposed to be higher than those of seated adults. It is not uncommon to see a mother push a child down time after time with the admonition "*Nofo!*" ("Sit!"). Toddlers are also trained not to go near the sleeping mats of their parents, not to talk, and above all not to cry when guests are in the house.

Attempts at early training are often accompanied by severe punishment. Erring children are sometimes slapped on the buttocks, legs, or face or switched on the legs or buttocks with brooms made of coconut leaf midribs or even with leather belts. Mothers usually administer the punishment, although belt whippings of older children by fathers is not uncommon. Threats that the *aitu* (ghosts) "will get you" are sometimes made, but the common deterrent to improper behavior is refusing to allow children to go out and play in the moonlight when all the other children are doing so. While youngsters may be reprimanded for making too much noise or for standing in the house, little is said about the very common practice of throwing stones or bullying smaller youngsters. Parents often resort to stone throwing themselves; a crying baby may receive a shower of small pebbles accompanied by shouts of "*Soia!*" ("Stop it!"), "*Uma!*" ("Enough!"), or "*Filemū!*" ("Peace!").

Up until the age of three, children retire after the evening meal and sleep with their mothers. At three, they are given a mat of their own and they must roll up the mat and fold their own sheets every morning. At this age children retire when their parents do—between nine and eleven o'clock. Parents are not rigid about their offspring's sleeping schedules and very small children are often allowed to stay up quite late when guests are present or when the family is attending a feast or a Samoan dance.

Up until the age of three or four the care and training of Samoan children is much the same for both sexes. At this time girls begin to assume certain responsibilities consistent with the female sex role, such as aiding in the feeding of younger children (although not exclusive care), running errands, and such other household chores as are within their physical capacity. Boys of the same age are given much more freedom. They rarely have to concern themselves with smaller children, but they may be called upon to feed chickens, fetch fresh water, or collect coral pebbles from the beach for *fale* flooring.

By the time a child reaches the age of seven or eight there are few chores to which they have not been exposed, be it light agricultural work, fishing or reef scavenging, cooking, or the processing of mat-making materials. A major responsibility for Fitiuta children is yard work. They pick up leaves that have fallen from the trees overnight, weed, and cut grass with bush knives. For a time, many of these duties are shared by both sexes, although boys continue to have much more free time for play than girls since they have less responsibility for caring for younger family members.

Samoan culture is characterized by a smooth and gradual coming of age process wherein children are increasingly given added responsibilities and more and more difficult physical tasks as they are capable of handling them. Being "too young" is never given as a reason for not allowing a child to undertake a given task. Whether it be the handling of dangerous tools, the carrying of extremely heavy loads of produce, or the maneuvering of outriggers in heavy surf, if a child thinks he can handle the activity, parents do not object.

But children also find time for play. They play cricket, tag, marbles, and a Samoan variety of hopscotch. They swim, pelt one another with Tahitian chestnuts, fashion toy sailboats out of sardine cans and coconut leaves, or make pull toys out of two tiny immature coconuts connected with a stick (like a bar bell). Playing with dolls, however, is not a Samoan pastime. Perhaps the leisure time activity most enjoyed is group singing and dancing. On moonlight nights (the best time for play) little clusters of children can be found on the village green (*malae*) singing and clapping in unison while one after another gets up to perform his or her version of the *siva*. When adults hold dances in connection with *malaga* entertainments, the chief spectators are always children who stand outside the house and offer their own imitations of what they observe going on inside.

Work and play patterns are, of course, greatly altered during the time that school is in session. Children enter school later than American youngsters (at about age seven). The Fitiuta schoolhouse in the very center of the village is likewise the very center of their lives from grades one through nine. The eight to two-thirty school hours monopolize a great deal of the children's time which might otherwise be devoted to learning and performing traditional work activities. Consequently, family patterns of labor have changed during the last generation, and adults are now required to perform many more chores than was necessary before the advent of formal education. Child care has been shifted more to the elderly during school hours, and now everyone must share the petty tasks once assigned to smaller children. While most families are convinced of the value of formal schooling, there are still many who keep children home from school when they feel they have need of them in particular work projects. This attitude is rapidly passing. There is a tendency, however, to regard education as being more important for boys than for girls.

In spite of numerous Western influences in Samoan life, some traditional customs related to childhood persist. The matter of circumcision is a case in point. This operation is an important milestone in a boy's life, an ordeal wherein voluntary submission proves a boy's bravery and prepares him for adult life. Girls look with disdain upon an uncircumcised lover.

At about age nine or ten a boy makes his own decision that he must submit to this operation. He arranges with a friend (*soa*) to accompany him and they

Samoan teen-ager.

seek out a native specialist (*tufuga*). Some go to a Samoan medical practitioner, but since none resides in Fitiuta, the traditional specialist is usually patronized. The operation is relatively simple and involves a minimum of pain. A pointed stick or piece of coconut shell is inserted under the foreskin and a single longitudinal cut is made with a straight razor, bamboo knife, or piece of glass. After this incision has been made, the boy bathes in the sea and his penis is dressed with the leaf of the *fanua mamala* (*Homalanthus nutans*) tree and bound with gauze bandages (formerly with white barkcloth). When the cut heals, the foreskin rolls back and the penis appears as if the foreskin had been removed; therefore this operation is not technically circumcision. Both the boy and his friend (*soa*) undergo the operation at the same time, and in some cases a whole group of boys will undergo the ordeal together. The *tufuga* is given gifts of food (cooked chicken, taro, breadfruit, and *palusami*) and barkcloth for his services.

The next important milestone in a young man's life is his entrance into the society of untitled men, the *aumaga*. This event used to occur at about age fourteen or fifteen (when he had completed nine grades of schooling), but today it occurs somewhat later since there is now compulsory high school education (the high school is in Ta'u village). First the young man must go to his *matai* and ask him to sponsor his request for membership. If the *matai* agrees he will go with the

Village taupou *lead the society of unmarried women* (aualuma) *in a group dance* (sasa siva).

youth to the village council. While the young man sits outside the house, his *matai* presents the assembled chiefs with a kava root in the boy's name, thereby asking official sanction of the body for the action the boy desires to take. When the council accepts the kava root, they are in effect giving the young man their blessing. Now he must prepare for his actual entrance into the *aumaga*. At the next meeting of this society of untitled men the initiate goes by himself to their meeting place with a gift of food known as *momoli*. This usually consists of a six-pound tin of corned beef plus other foods such as taro, breadfruit, and Samoan cabbage (*palusami*). After placing his food items in the middle of the floor, the initiate takes a seat in the back of the house and waits patiently until the matter of his induction into the group is reached on the society's agenda. Finally a speech of welcome is delivered by a *tamato'oto'o* (a Talking Chief's son who serves as the group's orator). The initiate must reply to his speech, and he then asks the group to share the food gift he has brought. A Talking Chief's son distributes the food and they all eat together, thus recognizing the novice as a permanent part of the group. The new member then takes a seat at a housepost corresponding to the rank of his family head. It will be in the front of the house if his *matai* is a Talking Chief and in the ends of the house if his family head is a Chief.

For teen-aged girls the important associational group is the *aualuma*. When this group functioned in traditional manner, it consisted of a group of unmarried women whose main function was to serve as a court to the ceremonial village princess, the *taupou*. They slept with her in a house called the *fale aualuma*, groomed her, served as her constant companions, and protected her virtue, for *taupous* were required to remain virgins. Membership in the *aualuma* is still a very important aspect of every girl's life, but the group no longer lives together and it no longer serves the *taupou*. *Taupous* are now appointed to serve on ceremonial occasions, and they are sometimes married women with children. In some villages the *aualuma* even includes the wives of untitled men, but in Fitiuta it is composed of unmarried girls (the youngest being about fifteen) and widows of all ages. The group comes together only on special occasions. The village may call upon the group to entertain a *malaga* with group dancing or they may be asked to raise money by weaving mats for some civic or church project. On such occasions the *taupou* is their official leader.

While both the *aumaga* and the *aualuma* engage in a great deal of community service, their members also have a good time. The societies have a social function much like college fraternities and sororities.

Fellow *aumaga* members often play an important role in a young man's courtship activities. Every young man needs an intermediary (*fa'asoa*) to play a "John Alden" role for him in approaching the girl of his choice and in arranging a rendezvous. Girls also have intermediaries, but they are less needed since boys are supposed to make the initial advances. Intermediaries for both boys and girls carry messages, arrange meeting places, give warning if a girl's brother is coming, settle lover's quarrels, and in the case of a very serious principal, propose marriage to the girl.

Ever since early voyagers discovered a sailor's paradise among the amorous maidens of Tahiti and Hawaii, all of Polynesia has had the reputation of being a place of free and easy sex codes which even Victorian missionaries could not reverse. Margaret Mead's description of Samoan premarital sexuality as involving "free and easy experimentation" may to some extent be true, but one might question her observation that "the concept of celibacy is absolutely meaningless to them" (1928:98). There are prohibitions against premarital sex activity and some of them undoubtedly predate the coming of the missionary. Village ceremonial maidens (*taupou*) have always been required to remain virgins, and when they were finally married, the wedding rites involved a defloration ceremony to provide public proof of that virginity. Similar restrictions are believed to have applied to other girls in families of high rank who were not *taupou*. Although against government law, a ceremony of this type was performed on a young woman of an elite family two years prior to the author's visit to Manu'a. Moreover, the Fitiuta village council imposes heavy fines on any family wherein a member gives birth to a child out of wedlock. Mothers *are* concerned about their daughter's sexual behavior, and there is much less freedom than has been sometimes described. If Samoa is the land of such sexual freedom, one is hard pressed to explain the necessity of the well-known *moetotolo* phenomenon. *Moetotolo* may be translated "sleep crawling," and is recognized as a form of rape which would seem to be unnecessary if sexual opportunities were as easy to come by as some observers claim. Considering that Samoans have little or no knowledge of contraceptives and that the illegitimate birth rate is not particularly high, one would be inclined to conclude that premarital sexual experimentation is probably no greater than that among American young people.

Samoan standards of beauty differ somewhat from our own. A Samoan male finds a young woman attractive who has a plump (but not fat) figure with firm, but not necessarily large, breasts, large but not muscular legs, long wavy hair, clear dark eyes with long lashes, full lips, good teeth, olive skin and graceful, well-proportioned hands.

Men marry at about age twenty-five and girls at age twenty. Samoan men and women marry because they need each other economically and socially, although there is a tradition of romantic love as may be seen in numerous myths and legends. Sina and Tigilao were romantic characters indeed and these and others often are represented in mythology as dying for love. There do indeed appear to be strong emotional ties between lovers and between husbands and wives, but there is much less emphasis on personal happiness as a reason for marriage than is to be found in Western cultures. While Samoan young people choose their own mates, marriage is definitely more of a family affair than a personal or individual affair. Samoans love children, and marriage is the proper institution in which to operate in order to produce them. Nearly everyone marries in Samoan society sooner or later, and the society is just not set up to support bachelors or spinsters either socially or economically.

THE WEDDING

Samoan weddings feature an exchange of a vast amount of property (*toga* for *oloa*) and the engagement period is always a busy one for both families involved. The origin of this institution of lavish gift exchange at weddings and a number of other important occasions is not known, but various students of Polynesian culture have speculated on the function it fulfils in the social organization. One position is that it adds some spice of life to an ordinarily humdrum existence. It is, so to speak, a matter of having Christmas several times a year with all the fun of receiving gifts and affirming the good will that exists between individuals and between families. Other observers see the phenomenon as being merely another economic system developed to promote the equal distribution of resources throughout the community. In a subsistence economy without enterpreneurs or markets where local products are sold, there must be a method of product distribution. Robert Maxwell sees the reported "generosity" of Samoan islanders as merely a means of dealing with surplus. Remembering that the *oloa* gifts given by the male's side of the family consist mostly of food, Maxwell's ideas concerning the exchange system seem sound. He maintains that in Samoa's climate "food spoiled quickly unless consumed. The food given to others was not forever gone. Sooner or later, others would have a surplus and would return in like amount. The effect

(Top) Samoan bride and groom. (Bottom) Bride and groom at wedding feast.

was that one's neighbors acted as storage bins for food" (1970:142). Whatever the reason for gift exchange, it continues to be a vital part of the system and one which consumes much time and conversation of families preparing for a wedding.

There had been a great deal of excitement in the village ever since Lemalu and Lise had announced that they would be married. In traditional fashion the announcement was made exactly two weeks in advance of the important day. The members of the *aumea mamae* (wedding party) were selected from among relatives and friends, and Lise's mother had been working for days on the wedding dress. The material was white satin shipped over from the store in Pago Pago and there was a veil of white lace. The dress was like one Lise had seen in a magazine and was cut out without a pattern and sewed on a hand-powered Singer sewing machine. Lemalu would wear his white cotton Sunday coat, a white lavalava, and white shirt and grey tie. He had ordered matching grey ties for the men in the wedding party, and the women in the party would all be wearing matching dresses of pastel pink and large flat straw hats.

The preparations of the extended families of the bride and groom were no less elaborate than those of the immediate families. Storage trunks in a score of *fales* were opened and the best of their cache of barkcloths, finemats, and lengths of floral print trade cloth were selected for the forthcoming event. Invitations to the wedding and a wedding feast had been mailed to relatives and friends in other villages or hand-carried to nearly every family in Fitiuta. The households of the bride and groom would share the expense and labor of a great wedding feast which would feature kegs of beef, cooked whole pigs, tinned corn beef, canned sardines and salmon, dozens of baked chickens, special traditional items like *palusami* (cooked young taro leaves and coconut cream) and *tafolo sami*, and prestige items like cakes with pink and green frosting and two-inch thick peach custard pies with formidable crusts. Other families would bring food offerings as well, and on the day preceding the wedding, columns of white smoke would rise from nearly every cookhouse in the village.

On the day of the wedding the *aumea mamae* gathered in front of Lise's house. Soon the groom joined them and, after a few last-minute adjustments of her veil, Lise came out and she and Lemalu led the wedding party in a double column off through the village. Their destination was the home of the district Samoan judge. When they reached his *fale* everyone crowded inside and sat on the floor mats. The judge read a civil ceremony, pronounced the couple "man and wife," and gave them his blessing. From here the wedding party went to the church where before an assembly of family and friends the village *faifeau* (pastor) performed a second marriage ceremony—this time a religious one.

Following a ceremony much like that performed in a Congregational church in the United States, the wedding party, families, and friends moved to a large grassy spot in the center of the village where a framework covered with coconut fronds had been built to shade the guests at what would be a lavish wedding feast. Two long parallel rows of mats had been laid down, and between them had been set a long row of leaf baskets overflowing with food. Little boys armed with coconut branches stood by to shoo the flies. At the suggestion of a Talking Chief from Lemalu's family, all the guests found a spot on the mats and sat cross-legged while a series of village chiefs gave speeches welcoming everyone and wishing the newlyweds well. After the *faifeau* gave "thanks to God," everyone began to eat from the leaf baskets before them. As usual, there was much more food than could be consumed by twice the number of guests present. Shortly after the meal began, little boys arrived with coconut leaf baskets and each of the guests began piling great quantities of the food into these containers. The food would be taken home so that it could be shared with those who had not been able to attend the festivities.

As the meal proceeded, there was joking and laughter. One of the old chiefs, an uncle of Lemalu, stood up and began to dance a ludicrous dance. Everyone clapped in rhythm and sang in order to encourage him. Soon dancers were getting up everywhere. Some of the young men ran to a nearby *fale* to get their guitars. Soon the feast was transformed into a dance and everyone moved into a nearby house. First the members of the groom's family danced, and then they challenged the bride's family to match their efforts.

All of a sudden, a great cry went up outside the house. The words "Mua O" were being shouted by a score or more of voices. Thirty young men came running down the path dressed in bright barkcloth costumes. It was the village *aumaga* arriving in a group to honor Lemalu, one of their own. The group formed into ten lines three deep. Their drummer positioned himself in front of the group with his percussion instrument, an empty kerosene can and a stick. He began a steady vigorous rhythm on the can and at a signal from him, the *aumaga* began their *sasa siva*. In Samoan, *siva* is the word for dance and *sasa* means "to strike." Thus the choreography involved the men clapping their hands together, slapping their bodies in unison, and going through a long series of coordinated dance movements —always in rhythm and always in concert. They squatted down, leaped high in the air, turned slowly in a full circle with one arm outstretched, slapped their thighs, made the motion of paddling a canoe, and another like that of throwing a spear. The dance went on for about five minutes and ended in a great war whoop.

It was at this point that Talking Chiefs representing both families announced the gifts that were to be given. There were presentation and thank you speeches and much "ohing" and ahing" as the gifts were produced and taken to the houses of the two families. The gifts went to the families and not to Lemalu and Lise, with the exception of a few linens and lengths of trade cloth for *lavalavas*. After the gift exchange, the young people began the dancing again and this went on far into the evening, the jubilation being materially aided by several gallons of "home brew," a special contribution of the *aumaga*.

When the long day was over, the newly married couple went to Lemalu's household where the family had made them a special place to sleep. Barkcloths had been hung up to form a separate room apart from that occupied by the rest of the family. The next morning Lise would begin her life as a housewife—working

Aumaga practicing its group dancing for the forthcoming wedding celebration.

with the other women of Lemalu's household. Samoan custom does not include the concept of a honeymoon.

DOMESTIC LIFE

While in the case of Lemalu and Lise the couple took up residence in the home of the husband's people, there is free choice as to which side of the family a newly married couple will live with. There is no such thing as neolocal residence, that is, establishing a home separate from either family. Where the couple will live seems largely dependent upon where the husband seems to have the best chance of succeeding to a *matai* title. If the wife's family has a shortage of men, there is excellent opportunity for a young bridegroom to establish himself as a vital contributing member of that household and therefore be a frontrunner for election to a title in her family should one become vacant. If the young man, on the other hand, is the eldest son of the *matai* in his own household, he would be likely to bring his bride to live with his people.

Regardless of where the bride and groom choose to live, their activities within the family are much the same. They must work with other family members in the cooperative labor of the household whether it be agricultural work, household chores, child care, or fishing activities. There is less leisure time for young women than for their husbands. Respite from a thousand and one household tasks comes only on Sunday afternoon when it is possible to relax and nap for a few hours between church services.

A wife's most important role is that of childbearer. Large families are always desired, for they insure an adequate labor force for family enterprises and they promise a leisurely old age for the parents. Samoans believe that the only natural state for an adult is to be married and to be a parent. Divorce is rare, but that does not mean that there are not a significant number of cases of marital discord. The lack of privacy in the Samoan household undoubtedly reduces the amount of overt conflict, and Samoans perhaps expect less of marriage than do Americans. Unhappy marriages are probably tolerated longer in Samoan culture than in America because personal happiness was not a major concern in the union in the first place. Legal divorces are rare, perhaps because they cost money, but separations are not. The chief grounds for divorce in Manu'a is adultery, and to be guilty of this indiscretion is considered worse for a woman than for a man. Cruelty and desertion are also grounds for divorce, as is laziness, particularly in the case of the wife. Children of a divorced couple tend to remain in the household where they have been residing and are visited infrequently by the parent who has taken up residence elsewhere.

Aumaga *dancers.*

Every adult male looks forward to the day when he will be elected to a *matai* title, but it cannot be said that untitled men are envious or covetous of the position of their family head. They work diligently and faithfully for the family and believe that if they are patient their efforts will someday be rewarded. When the time comes that a man's family or his wife's family selects him for a chiefly title, new responsibilities are taken on. A passage from Copp's book *Samoan Dance of Life* gives some insight into this new status:

> And so I got to be a *matai*. And I can't go often now and play cricket with my boy-gang or sing love songs along the road by the moonlight. And also, when a happiness-time is in the village, I can't sing and dance any more like I used to make them laugh, but I have to sit in my place and watch the company of young men sitting there in their own place and doing everything.
> And I'm sorry for this. But I'm glad too. Because now I am a real family Head, and I can sit with the other chiefs in the meeting *fale* and give my opinion too and have my share of food (1950:172–173).

*Matai*ship is the crowning achievement of middle age. Few acquire this status before their late thirties or early forties. It is a time of responsibility and service to family and village as a fully mature and capable adult, and it brings prestige and respect. The *matai's* wife likewise enjoys an elevation in status, and with it, an extra measure of responsibility. She now plays a decision-making role in the Women's Committee of the village, a role of equal importance to that her husband plays in the *fono*. In the household she is a fictive "mother" to all who live under her roof, and she directs the domestic activities much as her husband coordinates the family work in the fields and on the reef and sea. The *matai* and their wives are the pillars of Samoan society, the perpetuators of *fa'asamoa* (the Samoan way of life), and all in all, Samoa's solid citizens.

OLD AGE

Old age begins about age fifty when men are referred to as *toeaina* or *matuaali'i* (old man) and women as *to'omatua* or *olomatua* (old woman). Sometime within the next ten to twenty years the word *vaivai* (weak in the body) may be added, even if this is not actually the case. Old age is invariably identified by young and old alike as "the best time of life." It is a time when one is highly respected, when demands on one's time and energy are at a minimum, when most of life's taboos have been lifted, and when one can, if he wishes, sit back and let his children and relatives support him. Most Samoans, however, believe that extreme longevity is the result of working every day.

Samoa is not an unpleasant place in which to grow old. The climate is mild and permits maximum social contact and societal participation. The elderly are well integrated into their society and see themselves as valuable participating members in family and village enterprises. They enjoy interacting with young people and are often found working or just visiting with groups of young fishermen on the reef or with groups of young adult women engaged in mat weaving. Even the architecture of Samoa favors the elderly. Since the traditional Samoan house is open on all sides, old people need not even leave their homes in order to greet friends and neighbors as they pass on the path, and they are able to keep reasonably well-informed of much that is going on in the village.

One of the advantages of old age is a softening of taboos and an easing of the rigid code of etiquette that governs much of Samoan social and ceremonial life. The brother-sister avoidance requirements are no longer in force. Elderly siblings of the opposite sex are free to sit together for long hours enjoying each other's company without feeling ashamed or guilty. Moreover, in village council meetings special deference is shown to old chiefs and even the most intemperate of remarks is tolerated. The aged feel no compunction to maintain a dignified image and, in fact, they often play the clown at dances or other social gatherings.

Samoans feel that the aged have a right to engage in any form of labor of which they think themselves capable, and there is no stigma if they decide to do nothing at all. There are, however, a number of activities which are associated with the elderly and these tend to be sennit making, light agriculture, and reef fishing for men, and child care, mat and *siopo* production, sewing, and weeding the yard for women. Sex does not determine work activities as strongly as it does among

Processing laufala (*pandanus*) *in preparation for a mat weaving session. (Photo courtesy of William Short.)*

younger people, and old men seem to find no shame in helping their wives with domestic tasks and even with baby-sitting. Traditionally it has been the elderly who have generally been recognized as the most adept at bush medicine, massage (fofō), tattooing, midwifery, and story telling. One of the most important positions in the village—that of tu'ua (advisor to the village council)—is always reserved for an elderly High Chief. Retirement is a concept foreign to Samoa, although some chiefs upon reaching advanced age will give up their matai title, and there-fore their influential position in the village council, so that a younger family member may achieve recognition for a lifetime of faithful service to the family.

Life expectancy is much less in Samoa than in most countries of the Western world. The average age of death is 38.4 years, but because of a high infant mor-tality rate this figure is misleading. The percentage of Samoans who reach the age of sixty-five in Samoa is 2.7 while the figure in America is 9.3. Seriously ill people usually refuse to go to the hospital in Pago Pago, believing that if they should die away from home their spirits will be troubled and cause the family harm. They prefer to remain at home where relatives can be in constant attendance and the local nurse or Samoan medical practitioner from Ta'u village can make an occasional call to check on their progress and prescribe any needed medicines.

When a person dies in the home, all blinds which might have been lowered to shade the patient are immediately raised and a boy of the household is sent to toll the death on the bell in the village church. Members of the female branch of the family, the tamasā, immediately begin to prepare the body in full view of anyone who chooses to watch. This usually includes a throng of curious children. The corpse is dressed in white clothing and placed on a pile of sleeping mats which have been covered with a white sheet. Relatives in the tamasā branch of the family position themselves around the body and watch over it until it is removed for burial. The village pastor usually remains with the family to assist in any way he can. Grief is not excessive and there appears to be no retention of earlier practices reported by the first missionaries wherein mourners bruised their head with stones or cut themselves with sharp objects.

Within a short time after the announcement of the death, the church choir calls a rehearsal to prepare for their ceremonial visit (leo) to the grieving family. Within four or five hours of the death the choir arrives at the home of the deceased dressed in black, and is seated within the house. A few hymns are sung, and a speech for the dead (lauga i maliu) is delivered by a choir member (usually a Talking Chief). This visit is made with the express purpose of consoling the family and therefore a representative of the family must respond with a speech, thanking them for their thoughtfulness. After the exchange of speeches another hymn is sung and the choir departs.

As long as the body remains in the house, the women of the family will never leave it. They are forbidden to sleep, and if one of them should nod off, ashes will be smeared on her forehead which cannot be washed off until after the funeral. Throughout the long night young men from the village come in to play guitars and sing so that the relatives will find it easier to stay awake. Because corpses are not embalmed, and because this is a tropical climate, burials normally take place within twenty-four hours of death. In the meantime, messages must be sent to other villages and within a few hours relatives and friends of the family begin to arrive with gifts of trade cloth, *siapo*, and finemats. If the deceased is a chief, there will probably be a considerable show of wealth, and this wealth, consisting mainly of finemats, will be displayed on the mosquito netting wires strung about the house. The chief's family provides one large and particularly valuable finemat (*afuelo*) which will hang just behind the body. After the funeral this treasure will be given to the female relative who has taken care of the cleansing and the dressing of the corpse.

The family head selects the grave site somewhere on the village land of the household. In the case of a deceased family head, the site is chosen by another influential titled member of the family. The grave is dug by members of the deceased's family aided by friends. If the dead man is titled, fellow chiefs will dig the grave and will receive a special payment (*lafo*) for their labors after the funeral. The body is wrapped in the sleeping mats, sheets, and *siapo* on which it has laid in state and is carried to the grave site by members of the village choir or members of the household. Graves are dug in two levels, and the corpse is placed in the bottom level in preparation for the funeral service.

The funeral service, much like one in a stateside Congregation church, is read by the village pastor (*faifeau*) with the family, friends, and church choir at graveside. The choir closes the service with a hymn which says "Tofā, Tofā" ("goodbye, goodbye"), and the pastor and mourners throw three handfuls of sand apiece into the grave. When the mourners have left the grave side, sheets of galvanized iron are placed over the lower level of the grave which contains the corpse. The metal sheets are weighted down with heavy rocks and sand is shovelled into the grave. The grave of a titled man will usually be marked with a rock cairn or a headstone of poured concrete, but the grave of a woman, an untitled man, or a child will be marked only with a coral slab. The grave will be supplied with flowers for a year and then forgotten.

Following the funeral the mourners are fed and given food to take with them to their homes. Special shares of pork, chicken, fish, and taro are set aside for the *faifeau* and all other friends who assisted in the burial. Special care is taken to reimburse the donors of finemats and *siapo* by giving them food and other goods of equal value. Some of the finemats will be given as *lafo* to village chiefs and to the pastor for services rendered, and the rest will be stored away until there is another death in the village and once again every family is expected to bring their gifts of sorrow and respect for the deceased.

6 / The changing Samoan world

Most anthropologists who have worked in Samoa are impressed with its
extraordinary cultural conservatism. Douglas Oliver, for example, described this
island group as:

> presenting a radically different picture from the usual South Seas spectacle of
> native peoples cheerfully and unknowingly losing their identity and their
> heritage in a setting of successful and expanded economy established and
> controlled by white men (1961:220).

Oxford and Cambridge geographers, in a handbook titled *The Pacific Islands*,
singled out the Samoans as a "people with such a conservative nature that . . .
new elements (foreign goods, money, Christianity) have never been allowed to
sweep the land with the devastating effects to be observed in some other Pacific
island communities" (1943:608).

In a time when even the most isolated of primitive peoples are rapidly losing
their cultural identity in favor of Western ways, the Samoans are an enigma,
particularly when one surveys other Polynesian societies. Descriptions of the way
of life of islanders in the Northern Cook Group, an area where inter-island boats
call as seldom as four times a year, include such statements as, "The old types of
canoes have completely disappeared." "Houses are now made of sawn timber."
"Changes in the culture of the people due to European influence have been considerable" (Geographical Handbook Series:552–559). An island group farther
east, the Marquesas, is described as a place "where much of the native culture . . .
has disappeared" (Geographical Handbook Series:271).

Even the remote and sparsely populated atolls of the Tuamotu Group have
undergone sweeping changes. The traditional culture of the island of Raroia, for
example, is almost completely gone. Danielsson tells us that

> changes have been profound. . . . The material culture is almost wholly Western,
> and the natives use European tools exclusively, dress in the European way and
> frequently have such luxuries as radios, bicycles and refrigerators (1956:104).

Even the untrained observer is aware that in places like Hawaii, Tahiti, and New
Zealand the traditional native culture is to be found only in adulterated form, if at
all, and then it is often maintained only as a tourist attraction.

The Samoan phenomenon of cultural stability therefore presents an interesting anthropological problem. Why has this island group during 150 years of European contact been able to retain much of the traditional way of life while other Polynesians have abandoned theirs in favor of the ways of the white man?

Keesing has suggested that Samoan conservatism results from the archipelago's "smallness, isolation, and tropical climate, together with the political rivalry of the powers (Great Britain, United States, and Germany) and the elements of disunity inherent in the native polity . . ." (1934:477). A careful analysis of Samoan history, however, establishes the fact that none of these factors is completely unique to Samoa. Samoa is no smaller in land mass or in population than many other highly acculturated island groups, and Samoa has probably been less isolated than most. Douglas Oliver has established that Samoa, Tahiti, and the Marquesas were particularly popular ports of call for a great many whaling ships working in the Pacific. In the year 1846, for example, seventy-two vessels called at Samoa and many stayed an extended period of time. Samoa was discovered in the late eighteenth century, roughly about the same time that other Polynesian islands were first visited by Captain Cook and other European navigators. Samoa was merely one of many island groups missionized between the years 1814 and 1836. Traders were also extremely active in Samoa from an early date. As a matter of fact, the largest trading concern in the Pacific, the Godeffroy Company, maintained its headquarters in Western Samoa between 1857 and 1878.

The colonial experience of Samoa may have been somewhat different from that of other Polynesian societies. Samoa was the object of a long and bitter struggle between Germany, Great Britain, and the United States for economic and political control. The continual courtship of the loyalty and political support of the people by these three powers over half a century should have resulted in as much or more change than any experienced by other island groups.

The answer to the question of why Samoa has managed to retain much of its traditional culture is believed by the author to lie within the nature of the culture itself, particularly in regard to its attitudes and institutions relating to family, government, and the supernatural. It is also believed that in most situations where two cultures, meet cultural change will usually be the greatest in those societies wherein the traditional system rewards the fewest number of people, that is, there will be less tendency on the part of the majority of people to cling to a system which rewards only a few when a new, more egalitarian system presents itself.

In most areas where acculturation has been marked—Tahiti, New Zealand, the Cook Islands, the Marquesas, Hawaii, the Tuamotus—the cultures placed great importance on primogeniture, senior lineages, and other forms of stratification. Furthermore, the few elite who profited from these arrangements were securely supported in their positions by religious sanctions in the form of *mana* and *tapu*. While the bulk of the population may not have liked the situation wherein only a select few enjoyed power and prestige, it was difficult to oppose a system which had the blessing of the supernatural.

When the white man first arrived in Polynesia it was mainly for the purpose of winning converts to Christianity. The white man's god was usually perceived as more powerful than Polynesian gods even by people of rank, for after all, this foreign god had provided his followers with magnificent ships, efficient weapons, strong and beautiful clothing, and a myriad of attractive trinkets and useful tools. Since very few people profited from the traditional social system and since the gods no longer threatened the rank and file if they no longer supported their traditional rulers or the system which put them in power, most central and eastern Polynesians turned to the ways of the white man as an avenue of achievement. Furnas suggests that in Hawaii, for example:

> The commoner was flattered, perhaps stirred, when the white *kahuna* (priest) finally got round to telling him that any native, of whatever social stratum, had a soul of which Christ was solicitous. Nothing in his pre-white culture had ever led him to consider himself important to anybody (1948:137).

In New Zealand, according to Barnett:

> the members of ranking families as a group resisted education, whereas those of lesser birth sought it and used it to lay the foundations for a new kind of leadership, one based upon the knowledge of the ways of the foreigner (1953: 405).

And Keesing adds that "a new standard of *mana* rose to rival that attained in forwarding the tribal purposes, namely that of accomplishment in *pakeha* knowledge and habits, and possession of *pakeha* goods" (1928:58).

In Samoa, things were very different. There were chiefs but they received their elite position not through primogeniture but through election by their extended family. All who were reasonably wise, efficient, hard-working, and loyal to family interests were eligible. Neither was there the concept of senior lines which gave special advantage to certain branches of the family. Grattan points out that "progress from untitled to titled rank is the normal aspiration sooner or later of most adult males" (1948:14). And Goldman comments that the Samoans "come close to broadening the concept of aristocracy to include the common man" (1970:262).

The appeal of this traditional system can readily be appreciated from the statement of a native informant who pointed out that, "In our system everyone can trace a kinship relationship to a king or at least to a High Chief." Furthermore, it is within the range of possibility that if he played his cards right, he could someday conceivably be elected to one of these High Chief titles if not to one that had once been a royal title.

Another important factor to be considered in regard to Samoa's conservatism is that religion was not part and parcel of the social and political system. In other words, it was possible for the society to accept another religion without affecting the status or authority of chiefs. Samoans speak of sacred *fono* rather than sacred chiefs. The *malae* in Samoa was a village green where the village council met to decide local and regional issues. The *marae*[1] in central and eastern Polynesia, on the other hand, was a place where priests conducted religious ceremonies. What was undoubtedly the most devastating influence for change on most Polynesian cultures—the coming of Christianity—had little effect on the social structure of Samoa, since Samoan culture had less invested in religious sanctions. Samoa had always been ruled by the will of men and not by the will of the gods or by men acting for the gods. Since Samoan chiefs had never claimed divine rights, the loss of traditional deities or religious concepts did little to alter their role and status within the society.

Homer Barnett has observed that "when cultures meet, the majority of those who switch their allegiances are individuals with the least opportunity for full participation in the most valued activities of their society" (1953:404). Samoan society allowed its members wider participation in social, economic, and political affairs than any other Polynesian group.

THE WINDS OF CHANGE

The point of the above discussion is not that changes have not taken place in Samoa, but rather that changes have been less cataclysmic and pervasive in Samoa than in other parts of Polynesia. Keesing believes that the history of cultural change in Samoa can be divided into the following periods:

> (1) 1830–1869—the period of Samoan-mission-trader equilibrium, when "the Samoan accepted those goods he wanted from the trader, and bowed to the voice of an evidently superior Deity";
> (2) 1870–1934—a period of "political and judicial changes in accordance with the will of alien authorities whose word was backed by warships and prisons"; and
> (3) 1934 on—a period characterized by "a set of influences that may broadly be called educational [which] have commenced to spread out from the urban centres, by way of the schools, and through the part-Samoan population" (1934:476).

The author suggests that, at least for American Samoa, a new era of cultural change began about 1961 with a revived interest in America's Pacific island territory by Congress and the deliberate subsequent attempt to mold the cultural and economic future of its inhabitants. This was a time when new ideas were developed and plans formulated regarding education, industrial development, and tourism by an energetic American governor with congressional support. It is the period of from 1961 to the present which will be the focus of the remainder of this chapter.

---

[1] *Malae* and *marae* are the same word, with slightly different meanings spelled differently in the two Polynesian dialects.

The new high school in Utulei, on the shores of Pago Pago Bay.

After an eight year absence from the islands, the author returned to American Samoa in 1962 and made the following observations:

Samoa had changed. The United States had tripled its appropriations. A new cluster of high school buildings (in Pago Pago) had made possible universal secondary education. Plans were under way for the establishment of an educational television circuit and for the construction of 26 elementary schools. But in spite of improved plane and ship communications, tourism had increased little because the island still had but one small government-operated hotel. The Samoan government seemed mainly interested in education and tourism however, for most villages still had their antique and inadequate water systems, and no effective facilities for sewage disposal. Samoans eliminated either on the beach or in the bush. Medical facilities were roughly the same as in 1954.

Prosperity had come to American Samoa. Because of employment in the new construction program and in a tuna cannery, Samoans had more money. Beer and soft drink consumption had soared. Bush stores sold a wide variety of European tinned food. Taxi-cabs and private cars were numerous and traffic was becoming a problem. Girls in the Pago Pago Bay area and even in outlying villages had begun to wear makeup and European hair styles; some of the younger ones were daring enough to appear in capri pants. Bay area children knew how to twist as well as to *siva*, and stereo phonographs were not uncommon household possessions. Tahitian rhythms could be heard everywhere; the governor, in an attempt to "retain the best of Samoan culture," had employed a Samoan-born nightclub entertainer and dance instructor from Los Angeles, California, who taught Samoan school children Tahitian dancing and drumming, to the irritation of the Samoan chiefs (Holmes 1964:446).

Even in isolated areas like Manu'a, changes in family structure were beginning to be evident. It could readily be sensed that there was a general lessening of the economic and political influence of the *matai* and greater opportunity for the individual family members to control their own affairs than had traditionally been the case. But all of these changes were minor compared to what was in store for American Samoa.

EDUCATIONAL TELEVISION

In November 1964 the Crown Prince of Tonga (now king) addressed a congregation of some 7000 Samoans in Pago Pago stating, "In ancient times the environment of Samoa and Tonga ended at the seashore of Samoa and Tonga. Today, the world is smaller. Now the whole world is our environment."

This statement would be truer for American Samoans than any indigenous population in the world, for unlike any other, they have been exposed totally to the most pervasive Western educational influence ever devised in a developing territory. That influence has been the educational television system established

The village of Fagatogo, the chief commercial and governmental center on Pago Pago Bay. (Photo courtesy of Pan American World Airways, Inc.)

in 1964 at a cost of nearly three million dollars. Now in full operation, the system brings 180 video lessons a week into classrooms in twenty-four government schools in Tutuila, Aunu'u, and Manu'a. In addition to the elementary and secondary school programming, the system also is used to teach Samoan teachers (after school hours) and to educate and entertain those past school age.

Credit (or discredit) for the establishment of the system must be given to Governor H. Rex Lee, who served American Samoa as chief executive from 1961 to 1967. Appointed originally to direct a crash program to rectify the ills described in a *Reader's Digest* article (Hall 1961) titled "Samoa: America's Shame in the South Seas," Lee immediately set about to produce what politicians might conceive of as a properly administered and developed territorial possession. After lengthening the jet air strip and blacktopping the main roads on the island of Tutuila, Lee turned his energies to the area of education, particularly to the problem which is most apt to disturb most administrators who do not speak the native language—the fact that the natives are not fluent in English. In order to upgrade the level of fluency in English in particular, and the educational quality in general, the governor decided to turn to educational television as the most economical, and, hopefully, the most effective means of improving a system in which most of the teachers were Samoans with little or no college training and with English competency which in many cases was little better than that of the children they were trying to teach.

First there was the matter of the hardware to be installed. In order to cope with the problem of having to broadcast a signal to twenty-four consolidated schools in all parts of the mountainous islands of Tutuila and Manu'a, the latter being sixty miles away, it was determined that the 226 foot transmitting tower must be located on a mountain peak. The 1603 foot summit of Mt. Alava, near Pago Pago, was selected as the site for this installation, and a $140,000 tramway system was built to transport the technicians to the lofty control room. Another problem centered about the fact that very few of the villages had electricity, and therefore power lines had to be installed to make the television operation practical. Margaret Mead dedicated a power plant on Ta'u island in 1971 signalling the completion of the electrification program.

Special teams of educational advisors determined that the new curriculum should emphasize language arts, science, mathematics, and social science. Since the teaching of language arts (mostly oral English) was seen to be the most important aspect of the new education, a specialist was brought in from New Zealand to establish a unique linguistic approach to English similar to that which had been successfully used to give European immigrants to Australia a quick but fundamental knowledge of the language.

The advent of television instruction did not mean that the Samoan classroom teachers would be dismissed. Their new function was that of an aid to television instruction and a catalyst to learning. Television presentations account for about twenty-five to thirty percent of the child's educational experience. Each televised lesson lasts about twenty minutes, and then the television is turned off and the

Samoan teachers take over. Supplementary exercises, or drills, developed at the broadcasting center, are administered by the native teachers. Ideally, these teachers fulfill a dual function: they provide feedback to the broadcasters, that is, they evaluate the effectiveness of the lessons for children whose culture and behavior they understand; and secondly, they are able to speak Samoan and therefore clarify concepts which students have difficulty in comprehending when presented only in English. Too frequent use of Samoan in classrooms, however, has always been frowned upon.

There has been an attempt to encourage interest in the Samoan cultural heritage. Courses like "Polynesian History," "Samoan Language Arts," "Living in the South Pacific," "Samoan Language and Culture," "Samoan Writing," "Samoan Reading," and "Living in Samoa" are an important aspect of the educational experience.

Adult educational programming is as important to our discussion of cultural change as is that produced for school children. Schools are open evenings to the public so that families without their own television sets can take advantage of the three hours of evening broadcasting. These evening programs consist of industrial films and travelogs, commercial programs (without commercials), and National Educational Television programs. Concerning the "somewhat dated" commercial programs shown for entertainment, one educator has observed as follows, "Samoans, discerning critics, have developed marked preferences for comedy shows and westerns" (Stoltz 1967:22). Locally produced shows for adults include those in English language instruction, public health education, agricultural information, and Samoan and world news broadcasts.

The new educational system of American Samoa is reported to have done marvelous things for the territory's nearly 10,000 school children. Daily attendance averages about ninety-four percent, and the high school completion figure is ninety percent. More and more high school graduates are going on to college in American Samoa or on the mainland. A community college, founded in 1971, has an enrollment of over 1000 students. This institution of higher learning has programs in the arts and sciences, in teacher education, in vocational training, and there is a nondegree continuing education program for adults.

ECONOMIC DEVELOPMENT

Fitiuta is less affected by modern industrial and commercial developments than most Samoan villages. This is in large measure due to its relative isolation. Without a harbor or docking facilities, and without accommodations for European visitors, there has been little permanent Western influence. There is no industry other than agriculture and that is largely of a subsistence variety.

In the entire Manu'a Group (six villages) in 1970 there were only 136 persons engaged in wage labor. This was six percent of the population. These 136 wage earners were almost exclusively employed in government positions with the school system, the health service, or the public works department. A few people clerked in village stores or were engaged on a family basis in the production of matting for shipment to Hawaii, but there was no manufacturing in the modern sense, no commercial fishing, and no large-scale agriculture for cash.

The island of Tutuila, on the other hand, had in 1970 a total of 4939 individuals in the wage labor force. This was twenty percent of the total population. While a large number of these individuals (3515) were employed as teachers, health service workers, public works employees, and clerical workers in a variety of government agencies, there was also a substantial percentage of Samoans employed by private enterprise. A Van Camp and a Star Kist fish cannery employed a total of 1100 Samoans. Others have found work at the Americana Pago Pago Hotel in various aspects of the tourist trade, in a Bulova watch factory, or in a Beatrice Foods dairy products plant. The government is presently negotiating with firms which would like to establish branches in Samoa for the production of steel wire, industrial gas, textiles and clothing, paint, and petroleum. An eighty acre site has been set aside as an industrial park near the airport at Tafuna as a future home for these and other industrial enterprises.

A weekly interisland motor vessel allows Fitiutans to travel to other villages and other islands, but Ta'u island is largely isolated from what is happening economically in Tutuila. The commercial ventures initiated in Tutuila are not possible in Manu'a because of lack of land for industrial use and because of the problems of transportation. On an island where everything must be ferried out through a dangerous reef in longboats to ships which must anchor offshore, one could hardly expect much in the way of commercial or industrial development. This situation has had the effect of drawing off those who want wage labor positions and leaving behind those who are content to engage in subsistence agriculture and modest cash cropping. This is the more conservative and usually the older element of the population.

THE CHANGING *MATAI* SYSTEM

The Samoan social structure is changing, but the extent of change and the degree to which it is altering the Samoan way of life is a matter of some debate. Robert Maxwell, who judges the change to be extensive, describes the family structure on the island of Tutuila as follows,

> Family heads, who previously commanded the distribution of wealth, now find themselves with a decreasing economic basis for their political authority. And they themselves are not unaware that their power is being threatened from all sides. . . . And their moral influence, even within their own families, is waning, as more youngsters move out from under their scrutiny and control and establish themselves as wage earners elsewhere (1970:145).

In many of these Tutuilan villages households include distant relatives who have moved in from the more remote areas to work in industry or for the government. Although the chief in whose household they reside is a kinsman, he often is not

Americana Pago Pago Hotel—part of Samoa's new image. (Photo courtesy of Inter-Continental Hotels.)

the *matai* to whom they owe primary allegiance, and his control over their actions and attitudes is often less than effective.

In outlying villages like Fitiuta, village councils are able to control the behavior of the local inhabitants through a system of fines imposed upon the family head of an erring individual, but in the more urban villages of Tutuila, councils do little of a punitive nature. Violations of law tend to become police matters rather than council matters. Pago Pago Bay area households are extremely fluid in composition. People come and go and rarely develop any sense of belonging or loyalty. Delinquency in the form of property destruction, truancy, pilfering, and drunkenness has become a major problem among teenagers. The High Court of American Samoa now employs a juvenile officer and special counsellors and has inaugurated new procedures to involve the delinquent's *matai*, and thus reinstate something of the *fa'asamoa* influence in the regulation of behavior of young people.

Typical of the attitudes of some of the young acculturated Samoans is the response Maxwell recorded when he asked a young schoolteacher if he would like to have a chiefly title. The educator commented:

> It seems to me that the chiefs of the clans are taking advantage of the people who don't hold titles: . . . It used to be that everyone in the family would work

and give their whole pay check to the chief, and he would distribute the money to the members of the family. But I would like to work and give the money away the way I want. I would not give it to the chief to distribute: . . . My family has asked me several times to try to get a title, and I say: "No" (Maxwell 1970: 144).

Another man, age 36, who worked in the Pago Pago area is quoted as expressing a similar opinion: "I don't want none of that chief stuff! Who cares about chief anymore?" (Maxwell 1970:145) Maxwell explains that this man came from a Tutuila village in which there were eighteen chiefs, but in only one family did the members share their food with the chief the way they did in the old days. The other seventeen families still give gifts of food and goods to their chiefs, but not the way they used to.

Maxwell believes that the breakdown in Samoan social institutions is the result of better transportation (both local and to mainland United States), increased education (particularly in the use of English), and a great influx of material items, plus the increasing capacity and desire to own them. He believes that American Samoa has made the transition from a subsistence to a money economy. While fifteen years ago every family had the manpower to raise all of their own food, "plantations" now go uncultivated because family members are off working for wages. The open market in Pago Pago is now an indispensable part of the economy, and many of the foods sold there are now imported from Western Samoa or Tonga.

FITIUTA FAMILY ECONOMICS

In Fitiuta, increasing influence of the West has altered many of the economic activities and values of the family, but thus far the *matai* system survives, if in modified form, as the foundation of Fitiuta social, political, and economic organization. The majority of Fitiuta *matai* continue to be supported by the farming and fishing activities of their household members, plus donations of money from family members working in Tutuila, Hawaii, or mainland United States. Average remittances from overseas relatives amount to $50 per month, and some *matai* receive as much as $400 per month from these sources. This kind of support strengthens the status of the extended family and its chief by permitting greater participation in status-conferring activities such as donating generously to the church, engaging in extravagant gift exchanges, or purchasing prestige goods such as radios, television sets, and refrigerators.

David Pitt (1970) has established in his study of Western Samoan villages that the *matai* system and other traditional institutions of Samoan society appear more than adequate to support economic progress. Whether in the recruitment of labor for cash cropping, in obtaining the cooperation of relatives in marketing enterprises, or in the encouragement of commercially minded young men by families who look to them as potential recipients of important chiefly titles, the traditional institutions of Samoa are capable of providing the necessary organization for future economic development.

The *matai* system has long been a target of much ethnocentric opinion. As early as 1884, George Turner wrote,

> This communistic system is a sad hindrance to the industrious, and eats like a canker-worm at the roots of individual or national progress. No matter how hard a young man may be disposed to work, he cannot keep his earnings. . . . The only thing which reconciles one to bear with it until it gives place to the individual independence of more advanced civilization is the fact that with such a state of things, no "poor laws" are needed (1884:160).

In Fitiuta economic changes are taking place, but within the *matai* system. An increasing number of families are allocating sections of family land to untitled heads of constituent biological family units. Apart from small donations for the support of the *matai* and periodical contributions for family obligations such as property exchanges or church tithes, these individuals are free to manage their own economic affairs. Several years ago checks issued by the government for copra production were made out only in the name of the *matai*. Today they are more often than not issued in the name of untitled men for copra produced on individual sections of family land.

If villages like Fitiuta are not as progressive as most Europeans would like to see them, it is not necessarily the *matai* system which should be held responsible. It is the Samoan value system in general. As Trussell has pointed out, "The Polynesian culture is rich in ceremonies and traditions that stress other values over making a buck" (1968:84). Or as the Samoans themselves have expressed it, "We may not be wealthy but we are happy with *fa'āsamoa*. We do not envy the rich European in his Cadillac. His money leads him only to trouble" (Pitt 1970:266).

Even in Tutuila, it cannot be said that a large percentage are in favor of the economic developments that are taking place. The fish cannery, for example, has never been a popular place to work. Some Samoans express great joy at being fired for inefficiency, as they can then go back to their *matai* having tried to make extra money for the family but having failed because of the factory's "unreasonable demands" on its workers. The cannery, however, has never had a shortage of workers, for many of the employees are Western Samoans who have been lured to Tutuila by the relatively higher pay scales of American Samoa. The majority of Western Samoans, however, are content with the cash-cropping opportunities available in their own country.

Margaret Mead (1928) has described islanders as being like willows which bend and swing to every passing breeze but do not break. It will be interesting to see if the conservative Samoan value system can continue to support Mead's view under the present whirlwind of European cultural influence.

EMIGRATION

One of the more important realities of modern Samoan life is that Samoans are leaving the islands in large numbers to take up residence in urban centers in Hawaii and the West Coast of mainland United States. It is estimated that nearly 40,000 Samoans now live within the states of Hawaii, California, Oregon, and Washington. Emigration of any import did not begin until 1951 when the Department of the Navy turned over the administration of the islands to the Department of the Interior. Men who were members of the Samoan Marine Guard, known as the Fita Fita, were given the option of retiring and being paid on the basis of their years of service or transferring to the regular Navy. A large number of men chose the latter arrangement and were transported along with members of their immediate family to bases in Hawaii and on the West Coast. A few even wound up at Brooklyn Navy Yard.

The departure of the Navy left American Samoa with serious economic problems. Gone was the $282,000 annual civilian payroll. Economics was largely responsible for the fact that over 1500 Samoans emigrated to the United States during 1952.

Samoans continue to leave the islands today although economic conditions have improved greatly. Motivations for migration include desire for well-paying jobs which will enable them to obtain material possession beyond their reach in Samoa, desire to obtain education for themselves or their children, and for some, desire to escape what they consider an oppressive traditional social system involving heavy obligations to *matai*. Some no doubt leave out of a sense of adventure and curiosity.

Samoans who have migrated earlier represent a source of temporary aid to the new migrant in obtaining housing, a job, and social contacts in the city. The Samoan church serves as a center of community life in the urban setting and there are a substantial number of vigorous Samoan congregations in Honolulu, San Francisco, and Los Angeles. According to Joan Ablon, who has made an extensive study of San Francisco Bay area immigrants:

> Samoans by and large have adjusted with relative ease to an environment that in total perspective could hardly be more different from that of their native islands. Few are returning, although many say that they will "retire" to Samoa (1971:386).

But some of these migrants do return to American Samoa, particularly some of those who went to the mainland for educational purposes. More and more upper-echelon positions in the island government are being opened up for Samoans with stateside college educations. These people have high prestige among their fellow countrymen and are without question agents of change. A few of those who have returned have accepted family titles and are contributing a new dimension to the philosophy and operation of the *matai* system. Even those Samoans who do not return to their native islands are affecting the culture of American Samoa. Many faithfully send home money for the support of the *matai* and for family enterprises. Having relatives in the United States has also proved to be a great incentive for travel, and a major source of prestige for any modern American Samoan family is to be able to send their family head and his wife to the mainland or to Hawaii for a visit. As the people of this island territory increase their measure of self-government there will undoubtedly be greater employment opportunities and therefore greater incentives for young Samoans with talent and good educations to see a vocational future in their homeland rather than in the United States. Hopefully they will feel at home in both worlds.

THE ENVIRONMENT

Increased industrialization and modernization coupled with rapid population growth has produced ecological problems. Prior to the government's program to modernize American Samoa, there was little environmental deterioration, and conservation of natural resources was not an issue. The relatively small population could easily support itself on family land with a minimum of agricultural labor, and there was no problem obtaining ample food from the sea. Since there was no way of preserving the fish, only as many fish were caught as would supply a family meal and perhaps also allow for a generous food gift to a neighbor.

Until relatively recent times sanitation and waste disposal problems were minor. Most materials Samoans used for day to day living were biodegradable. Houses were made of wood and leaves, food trays were woven from coconut fronds, banana leaves served as plates, the Samoan fork was a piece of bamboo, coconut shells served as water containers, produce was carried from the bush and stored in coconut leaf baskets, and body decorations consisted of flowers or colorful leaves. In a village like Fitiuta there were no cars, refrigerators, or other household appliances. In fact there was no electricity and no roads. Canned food (mostly corned beef from New Zealand) has been around for a long time, but not in such quantities that the cans caused much of a refuse problem. They did sometimes contribute to health problems, however, because empty tin cans often collected rain water and were excellent breeding places for mosquitos.

While Fitiuta has lost population in recent years through emigration, and although it has not been subjected to the industrialization and modernization influences evident in Tutuila, there are increasing environmental problems. New housing is often constructed with galvanized iron roofs which in time will rust and have to be disposed of, and there is now electricity in the village and a growing demand for television sets, refrigerators, record players, radios, and other household appliances. There is now a road between Fitiuta and Ta'u village. With no service people to repair the mechanical gadgets, many of these will soon find their way to the junk heap. Furthermore, there is now more money to buy Western items. Family members who are employed in wage labor positions in

Tutuila or the United States send home remittances to family *matai* which make the purchase of many of these goods possible. A new and different standard of living is emerging. More canned foods now grace the Samoan table, there is a great demand for canned beer and soda pop, and an increasing variety of glass, plastic, and metal utensils and dinnerware is being incorporated into the Samoan way of life. While Tutuila has a regular government operated garbage disposal service, the trash being used for land fill purposes, the problem of refuse disposal plagues all of the Manu'an villages.

Tutuila has very serious environmental problems. For the first time in Samoan history soil erosion has become a major concern. Much of this stems from the Western practice of baring all the soil before planting. Samoan slash and burn methods were less efficient but also less damaging to the hillsides in this high rainfall region. Increased road construction, often without consideration for natural land contours, also contributes to this erosion dilemma.

The operation of two large fish canneries in the Pago Pago Bay area has necessitated the presence of over 200 Chinese and Korean fishing sampans, and these boats have been a major source of oil and other toxic pollutants. In 1971 a special harbor division of the Public Safety Department (Police Department) issued 196 citations worth approximately $16,000 for the dumping of oil into the harbor.

Water systems are inadequate in nearly all Samoan villages. This is perhaps surprising in an area where the annual rainfall varies between 100 and 200 inches a year, depending upon the locality. But village catchment systems and pipelines were installed when the villages had much smaller populations. New methods of sewage disposal now being contemplated by the government threaten to put even greater demands on water resources. Some two and one half million dollars are now being spent annually to try and solve these problems.

Samoans are becoming alarmed by the rapid deterioration of their environment, and American Samoa now boasts an active chapter of the Sierra Club which was initiated by the governor, but now consists of a group of highly concerned local citizens. Samoan efforts in the protection of their environment have included a United States Youth Conservation Corps project in 1971 wherein two hundred Samoan young people cleaned up villages, cleared beach parks, and built recreational areas in nine locations on Tutuila, Aunu'u, and Manu'a.

THE POLITICAL FUTURE

When John M. Haydon was appointed Governor of American Samoa in 1969, he pledged that he would be the last appointed chief executive of this island territory. If and when the Samoans are permitted to elect their own governor, they will have achieved a substantial breakthrough in the direction of self-government. Although Samoans desire greater political control over their islands, American Samoans are content to remain within the American national sphere. They reject ideas of independence and also of consolidation with Western Samoan, undoubtedly on economic grounds. Without subsidization from the federal government, American Samoa would be hard pressed to survive financially. The annual operating budget for the territory is approximately twenty-two million dollars. American Samoans look at their struggling cousins in Western Samoa and are reluctant to share their economic problems. They are also not eager to cut off their opportunities for open emigration to the United States.

American Samoa now has a delegate-at-large in Congress, an elected legislature, and laws that protect Samoan land from alienation. The people also have opportunities for employment in professional and semiprofessional jobs at wages heretofor unheard of. While most American Samoans are critical of much that is imposed upon them as territorial nationals, they tend to move slowly and cautiously in choosing their own directions for change.

In old Samoa there was a sport for chiefs known as *seuga lupe* (pigeon-netting). The platforms on which chiefs stood while trying to snare these birds were often erected far out on the reef. On days when the surf was high there was always the possibility of being swept off the platforms if they were not alert. This situation resulted in a proverbial saying—*Seu le manu ae taga'i le galu* (Catch the pigeon but look out for the waves). The wisdom remains, if not the actual words, in the American Samoan national motto, "Progress with Caution." How else can a culture learn to bend with every passing breeze and not suffer a mortal fracture?

References

Ablon, Joan, 1971, "Retention of Cultural Values and Differential Urban Adaptation: Samoans and American Indians in a West Coast City," *Social Forces*, 49: 385–393.

Ala'ilima, Fay, 1961, *A Samoan Family*. Wellington, New Zealand: Islands Education Division of the Department of Education.

Barnett, Homer, 1953, *Innovation: The Basis of Cultural Change*. New York: McGraw-Hill, Inc.

Buck, Peter, 1931, "Samoan Chieftainship," *Hearings before the Commission Appointed by the President of the United States in Accordance with Public Resolution No. 89*, 70th Congress, Washington, D.C., pp. 70–73.

———, 1965, "Polynesian Oratory," in *Ancient Hawaiian Civilization*, E. S. Craighill Handy *et al.* Rutland and Tokyo: Charles E. Tuttle Co., Inc.

Churchill, William, n.d., *Fa'alupega*; *Manu'a*. Unpublished manuscript.

Copp, John D., 1950, *The Samoan Dance of Life*. Boston: Beacon Press.

Danielsson, Bengt, 1956, *Work and Life on Raroia*. London: George Allen and Unwin Ltd.

Furnas, J. C., 1948, *Anatomy of Paradise*. New York: William Sloane Associates.

Geographical Handbook Series, 1943, *The Pacific Islands Vol. II: Eastern Pacific*. Oxford and Cambridge: Oxford and Cambridge University Presses.

Goldman, Irving, 1970, *Ancient Polynesian Society*. Chicago: University of Chicago Press.

Government of American Samoa, Public Health Department, 1950, "History of Naval Medical Activities in Samoa," Pago Pago: Government of American Samoa, pp. 1–4.

Grattan, F. J. H., 1948, *An Introduction to Samoan Custom*. Apia: Samoa Printing and Publishing Company.

Gray, J. A. C., 1960, *Amerika Samoa*. Annapolis, Md.: United States Naval Institute.

Green, Roger, 1966, "Linguistic Subgrouping within Polynesia," *Journal of the Polynesian Society*, 75:6–38.

Hall, Clarence, 1961, "Samoa: America's Shame in the South Seas," *Reader's Digest*, July, pp. 111–116.

Heyerdahl, Thor, 1950, *Kon-Tiki*. Chicago: Rand McNally.

Holmes, Lowell, 1964, "Fieldwork Report: Leadership and Decision-Making in American Samoa," *Current Anthropology*, 5:446–449.

Howells, W. W., 1933, "Anthropometry and Blood Types in Fiji and the Solomon Islands," *Anthropological Papers of the American Museum of Natural History*, 33:279–339.

———, 1967, *Mankind in the Making*, Rev. ed. Garden City: Doubleday & Company, Inc.

Keesing, Felix, 1928, *The Changing Maori*. New Plymouth, New Zealand: Thomas Avery.

———, 1934, *Modern Samoa*. London: Allen & Unwin, Ltd., and New York: Institute of Pacific Relations.

Maxwell, Robert, 1970, "The Changing Status of Elders in a Polynesian Society," *Aging and Human Development*, 1 (2, May):137–146.

Mead, Margaret, 1928, *Coming of Age in Samoa*. New York: William Morrow and Company, Inc.

———, 1930, *Social Organization of Manua*. Honolulu, Bishop Museum Bulletin No. 76.

Milner, George B., 1966, *Samoan Dictionary*. New York: Oxford University Press.

Oliver, Douglas, 1961, *The Pacific Islands*, Rev. ed. Garden City: Doubleday & Company, Inc.

Pitt, David, 1970, *Tradition and Economic Progress in Samoa*. New York: Oxford University Press.

Stoltz, Jack H., 1967, "Educational TV in a Pacific Paradise," *California Teachers Association Journal*, Oct., pp. 18–22.

Trussell, Tait, 1968, "Trouble in Paradise," *Nation's Business*, 56 (July):82–87.

Turner, George, 1884, *Samoa a Hundred Years Ago and Long Before*. London: Macmillan and International Ltd.

Wilkes, Charles, 1845, *Narrative of the United States Exploring Expedition during the Years 1838–1842*. Philadelphia: Lea & Blanchard.

Williams, John, 1832, *South Seas Journals*. London Missionary Society Records (on microfilm) at Ablah Library, Wichita State University.

Williamson, Robert W., 1924, *The Social and Political Systems of Central Polynesia*. Cambridge: Cambridge University Press.

Worsley, Peter, 1957, *The Trumpet Shall Sound*. London: Macgibbon & Kee, Ltd.

Recommended reading

Gilson, R. P., 1970, *Samoa 1830–1900: The Politics of a Multi-Cultural Community*. Melbourne: Oxford University Press.
Ethnography and history integrated into a single study of the Samoan islands as influenced by the struggle for power of Great Britain, Germany, and the United States.

Grattan, F. J. H., 1948, *An Introduction to Samoan Culture*. Apia: Samoa Printing and Publishing Company.
Ceremonial life and social structure in Samoan society.

Gray, J. A. C., 1960, *Amerika Samoa*. Annapolis, Md.: United States Naval Institute.
Excellent history of white contact in the Samoan islands, particularly the role played by the U. S. Navy in American Samoa.

Holmes, Lowell D., 1958, *Ta'u, Stability and Change in a Samoan Village*. Wellington, New Zealand: Polynesian Society (Reprint No. 7).
Study of cultural dynamics in Manu'an culture from 1836 to modern day.

Mead, Margaret, 1969, *Social Organization of Manua*, 2d ed. Honolulu, Bernice P. Bishop Museum Bulletin 76.
Monograph dealing with the formalistic aspects of Manu'an social and political organization.

———, 1972, *Coming of Age in Samoa*, Laurel ed. (paper). New York: Dell Publishing Company.
Classic psychological study of adolescent girls in Ta'u village, American Samoa.

RECOMMENDED AUDIO-VISUAL AID

Fa'a Samoa, The Samoan Way (17 minute sound, color film). Photography and narrative by Lowell D. Holmes. Available from Documentary Films, 3217 Trout Gulch Road, Aptos, California.
Housebuilding, fishing, cooking, and ceremonial life in Fitiuta, the subject of this book.